19.50

AIRYMOUSE

AIRYMOUSE

by

HARALD PENROSE

Illustrated by

PHILIP TREVOR

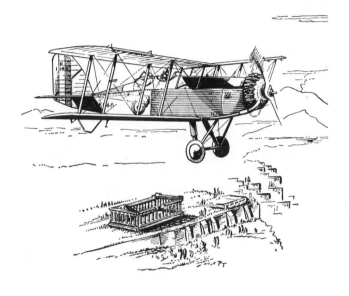

Airlife
England

This Edition published in 1982
by Airlife Publishing Ltd.
First Edition published in 1967
by Vernon & Yates

ISBN 0 906393 16 7

Airlife Publishing Ltd.

7 St. John's Hill, Shrewsbury, England.

Printed by Livesey Limited, Shrewsbury, England.

Contents

For Ian, who has explored the sky world with me and will understand that most of the incidents described are the highlights among many hours, when the pure enjoyment of flight itself has counted more than its little adventures.

'We have a very little time. Before we have reached the middle of our time perhaps, but not long before, we discover the magnitude of our inheritance. Consider England. How many men I should like to know, have discovered before thirty what treasures they may work in her air? She magnifies us inwards and outwards; her fields can lead the mind down towards the subtle beginning of things; the tiny iridescence of insects; the play of light upon the facets of a blade of grass. Her skies can lead the mind up infinitely into regions where it seems to expand and fill, no matter what immensities.'

HILAIRE BELLOC

I Remembered in Tranquillity

Silhouetted against the fiery sky of evening, the hill-top loomed high and lonely. A strong breeze rustled and flattened its tall grasses, and pale above the swaying tree-tops a full moon already ghosted. As the sun sank lower the level light suffused the countryside with brilliance that illuminated every hedge and tree and drew long shadows across the fields. Borne on the rasping air, the far thin song of many birds blended with the near and clear, mounting into a great evening chorus.

The wind whispered, cajoled, tempted: 'Lean on me: feel the upsurge; see how the homeward flying rooks revel in this buoyant lifting. I could rediscover for you the joy of flight above a timeless earth. It can be yours. Try!' . . . . And I listened, half believing I might escape the crazy world, forget the toppling idols, and find the old, wild gods once more. Slowly I scanned the vista: only empty echoes of ancient ways, and ghosts of cherished things were there.

As I listened to the birds, thought flew down the years. I saw myself at the beginning—expectant, curious, gazing from the half shadows of sheltered youth at new day pouring a path of light into the distance, where imagined voices sang as though there were neither bondage nor suffering in the beckoning world. The next two decades revealed such wealth of time for everything: time to spend without counting the hours; time to experience; to sail, fly, explore; time to love, to wed, to found a family; time to study and time to watch the steady swing of the stars; time to rest, and sleep in sweet oblivion. Suddenly time had three quarters gone: the family grown: days of adventuring become a dream. So with all men. Presently hidden questioning begins. Each day seems briefer. Old longings make nonsense of security and success. Away on the horizon the wild gods beckon for the last time. Soon it will be too late. Man gives a tug at his chains and fetters, hearing his doom in their clatter. If he does not, then his heart is already dead. With me there was the tolling of a distant bell. I had aspired and lived my summer; autumn was at hand. Soon there would be only winter for remembering—but I knew that I would take that same far path if there could be a second chance.

'You can,' whispered the wind. 'You can. Why sit at a desk tied with no break? It is restless exchange for a pilot's seat. Why not recapture those earlier days when you swept great curves through the skies as you watched the quiet world? All you need are wings.'

On my great hill the low, level rays seemed to renew my yesterdays, spanning the scenes I had known: those peaceful hills; the sequestered meadows bounded by network hedges and tall elms; brooks and little rivers filled with unpretentious purpose as they brimmed towards the sea. High in the sky above this quiet pastoral I spent my days—days and months that mounted to years, patterned with sunlight, shadow and cloud; questing through fog and rain; soaring blue heights that discarded the world and glimpsed infinities. Yet always there was the earth, the fair attractive earth, to which one must return: the close contacts of sight and smell and sound; the need to touch, to love.

Preceding my current task, there had been twenty-five years of testing many types of aeroplane, giving a freedom granted to few. In the lonely places and the high there was liberation from man-kind's complexities. I learned how frail the fallibility of life: how precious each hour. It was not the sun and the rain, sea, earth and sky themselves, but what they engendered in the mind that made reality. I was immeasurably enriched. Then it had ended. Only memory remained.

Though I have flown over many countries enthralled by individual facets of their sculptured form, it is the land of England that holds my heart—a green land with sunlight filtering through cloud rifts, brushed and tinctured by a thousand mists, her fragile littleness set like a lily leaf upon the vast waters of the globe. From the skies I see her substance as though risen from the matrix of the world, shaped by tropic heat and icy cold, scarred by over-flooding larva and smoothed by centuries of glaciers. Where once the sea encroached, hills that were islands lift vales of verdant fields threaded by brooks which are the last trickle of river channels anciently navigable. Where distant uplands stand smooth and bold above vanished swamps and forests, Stone-age man lived under the open sky.

The great wind blowing across my hill was like the rush of air cascading round the windscreen as I flew on wings of fantasy. From the same skies where eagle and fork-tailed kite soared above the first true colonizers of this land, I stare bemused at faintly shadowed mounds and silted ditches made by long forgotten implements of stone and bone. Echoes of the ancient past drift up: laughter, shouts of triumph, incantations mystic with need of heavenly life to ease the tragedy of this. Below me, civilization dawned and developed through an initiating two thousand years, until the great warmth and heavy rains that nurtured it changed to a colder and drier world, and the mighty builders of Avebury and Stonehenge fell powerless before the terrifying metal of bronze-armed conquerors infiltrating across the Channel, who presently absorbed Neolithic man. Centuries passed, and from the air I see the domed burial mounds of their chieftains, and the spectral outlines of fields and isolated farms overlayed by greater ditches made by a new influx of people armed with spears of iron against which bronze weapons were no match. In the age of warmer climate that temporarily returned, these Celts increased until they were a great tribal organization living in vast, many-ditched fortresses of gleaming chalk crowning the same hill-tops where the forgotten Neolithics lived and died.

In imagination I refocus my vision. Earth signs of successive civilization are everywhere—but they are memorials now. The fires are out, roofs of pit huts fallen in; the high places again deserted, except for an occasional freshly banked, square look-out where a new invader has come from Rome, and gazes across the farmsteads of his British vassals. Straight and magnificent road-ways are set arrow-like across the land—broad and strong for quick movement of legionaries and swift passage of commerce between principalities and towns which still make the framework of the England of today. From the skyways all is there, set indelibly across the face of the land. Anglo-Saxon villages of the next invasion turn their back on Roman roads, preferring valley mud-tracks which eventually became the rolling English road. Even before the Norman set his architectural seal, the landscape had acquired that final character and aspect of arable and meadow set among the heath and downland, made beautiful with copse and wood.

I know that man is dust upon the ancient hills. Roman, Saxon and Norman are whispering ghosts. In the neatly tended fields beneath imagination's wing the marks of all their centuries show, emphasizing that each man is tenant for so short a span of years. Tall spires dream above his grave, and on the village green a new generation of children play. The burning question of today becomes a hollow echo, and the profound truth a symptom studied by students of tomorrow. We live and love and are for-gotten—yet the power of man is inextinguishable and eternal for better or for worse.

Winging my subconscious thought with dreamlike flight across this western England which I know more intimately than any man before—not by name of town, nor from trammelled roads and path, but viewed harmoniously and whole—I watch the passing passage of rounded hills and far spread fields, smoke-drifted townships or sleeping villages, and find each feature fitting into place with a thousand other manifests of life. In quietness the land lies waiting as though prescient with understanding, no longer indifferent. I fly on with stillness of spirit; mind and heart at peace. Here is the immortal pattern, the unchangeable, eternal good earth whence all life rises and returns; yet by paradox a primitive earth, terrible but attractive, source of shelter and food, enemy as well as friend of life. And man dreams on, contemplating the mystery, pondering the significance, finding hell and heaven in his earthly paradise, while the world spins inexorably—an insignificant planet pent with passions in a vast universe of other suns and worlds in thousands and millions stretching outward beyond comprehension.

Thought unfolded thought as I rested on the ancient hillside. The sun touched the horizon's rim, flooding the waiting countryside with last rich hue. Through the level evening light thought soared above an earth grown glorified and golden. Soon dusk gathered on the glowing fields. The summer moon rode boldly high above the quilted trees, and the first pale stars gave mystery to the darkening sky. I sat there still remembering, while the soft wind flowed endlessly into the moonlit night. The world grew quieter still. Lights began to prick the dark loom of the land, and the sky grew silver with the lifted moon. But on the steady flood of the warm west breeze I was flying past the stars, seeking as of old the phantom music of freedom's wings.

2 *The Wings Aspire*

After that evening on the hill I became a student of advertisements —with the result that six months later I obtained, for the price of a large sailing dinghy, a diminutive single seater aeroplane of insignificant horsepower. Her name was *Airymouse*.

Brittle sunshine was already drawing long shadows across the airfield when I arrived to try her one February afternoon. With an air of demure innocence she waited alongside a veteran Tiger Moth whose wider wings seemed to dwarf her. For a moment I stood admiring with amusement the compact neatness of my tiny acquisition, wondering if this gaily painted toy could really rediscover the freedom of the skies.

Compared with the large and powerful metal aircraft I used to fly she seemed a fragile creature, yet the integrity and balance of her wood and fabric construction was evident enough. Nevertheless, she was an anachronism. Though her modern contemporaries were sleek little cabin monoplanes *Airymouse* was a biplane, crisscrossed with cable bracing that made her more romantically ancient than anything designed in the last twenty-five years. If she could fly in the same delightful manner as those light-winged, aerial creatures of old I would be more than satisfied.

I glanced into the old style, open cockpit. It boasted only air-speed indicator, altimeter, and cross level bubble for flight instruments, with tachometer and oil gauge for the engine. How different from the last airliner I handled—where tiers of ultra-violet illuminated instruments told not only of the functioning of turbines and mechanisims but interpreted balance and orientation to save disaster from man's misleading senses when skies were blind with cloud and fog. No pilot on his own could fly that machine, nor any other transport or bomber. A crew is required to integrate the complex systems. Even the pre-flight check of controls and cocks and switches took fifteen minutes listing against a reference book. When at last the airport Tower gave clearance to take-off, and the banked throttles were opened, we thundered down the runway gathering speed fully a mile before the moment was right to give a determined tug on the elevator to get us airborne.

The synthetic glass armour enclosing the crew's pressurized compartment became a cocoon insulating us from the reality of flight in the form we knew of old. Instead, the earth was disregarded for a grid of radio waves spelling safe pathway for the metal Juggernaut thrusting heavily into unfelt space as though on rails. In the cabin behind us the passengers turned to their magazines, bored with the dull panorama of endless cloud hiding a forgotten world, unaware they had relinquished destiny and lives to our dispassionate care, and not dreaming that either we or the intricate machine was fallible. But in the open cockpits of old the buffeting lift and surge of the wind made us one with the elements, as though the very spirit of flight in all its beauty and hazard was being experienced and understood. We were masters of our destiny instead of slaves to electronics. So I decided to turn the pages back, and bought *Airymouse* as token of earlier days.

The soft evening breeze touched her scarlet wings, and I imagined they responded with a scarcely perceptible, rapturous sway. Almost eagerly, I pulled on coat and helmet, and climbed into the red-cushioned seat of the stark little open cockpit so reminiscent of an ancient sports car. Located for safety, and minimum obstruction of view, it was placed well aft, just behind the centre section struts. Having strapped up the belt I moved each control to check freedom and correct rigging, then turned on the petrol. There was no self starter. The inescapable ritual began.

'Switch off. Suck in.'

'Switch off. Suck in,' I replied, and watched them turn the propeller, then stand poised for a swing.

'Contact.'

'Contact,' and I switched on. The propeller was flicked over compression. The engine failed to fire.

'Switch off.'

They tried again. Nothing. I hoped this wasn't indicative of endless starting trouble. Try once more . . . With a heavy shudder the two-cylinder engine fired and settled into a staccato tick-over, throwing a little avalanche of wind against my face. A myriad vibrations danced through the structure. Every wire thrummed up and down. Presently the engine was warm, and after a full-power run I waved away the chocks that held the wheels.

She taxied out with confidence, the rubber-cord springs, which tied the straight axle to the undercarriage apex, cushioning the miniature scooter wheels with surprising ease as they bumped across the tussocky ground. Recollecting how uncontrollable were some machines before the invention of differential brakes, I was prepared for difficulty in steering, but *Airymouse* gave ready response to blasts of slipstream against her deflected rudder. I was relieved to find she had not the slightest tendency to tip on her nose under those sudden surges of power—a characteristic that was to stand me in good stead in subsequent days of landing, whether by purpose or accident, on very rough ground.

At the far end of the field I ruddered until the orange windsock, lightly flying from a pole in the nearby hedge, showed we were aligned into what faint breeze there was. Framed in the rectangle formed by the boxed wings and struts, a prairie-like immensity of worn and rutted turf and mud stretched so far that neither boundary hedge nor tree could be seen. Above the empty distance slow clouds floated in a wash of sky from which the first hint of night was beginning to bleach the blue. I looked upward, where the centre-section trailing edge was cut away to give a better view, and saw the topmost heights still held their azure. Already the warp and weft of different experience had begun to cloak me. It is a familiar miracle to all who fly: a transformation in which the life throbbing through the machine's structure becomes part of one's own. A psychological door opens and there is sudden awareness that the moment of demarcation is poised at this instant between the now we live in and the limitless unknown beyond.

Green from the Control Tower. Reaction was like releasing a sprinter tensed for the gun. Automatically I glanced over my shoulder, and then ahead to see that the skies were clear. Compelled by the steadily opening throttle the two opposed cylinders shake and jump as *Airymouse* rolls forward enveloped in her miniature thunder. Gently as a breath, I press the stick a little forward, and her tail lifts on the slipstream, setting the wings at a shallow angle to help her accelerate. Like a skittish pony she tries to veer, but with a swift footstab is curbed by the rudder to counteract the slewing swirl of the slipstream. Run straight, my little creature! I can sense your purpose and feel how buoyantly you lean upon the wind, for your wings are part of me and growing lighter, more aerial, every second.

I had forgotten how lengthy was the run of the motor-cycle engined light planes of forty years earlier. In this gentle wind *Airymouse* took over three hundred yards to attain the necessary 40 m.p.h. for her take-off. I could feel she was drawing her utmost diminutive power to nerve her into flight. It was like setting a pony at a jump. With infinitesimal pressure I lift her. The patter of wheels changes to light rasping through the grass . . . and lo! she is free of the ground, floating insecurely on a rushing tide of air as she struggles into a climb almost beyond her strength. A grotesque, winged shadow chases her along the turf, slowly separating. In half a mile of *phuta — phut — phut* from the shaking engine *Airymouse* has crept to a height of only 150 feet. It was the old exciting game of pitting wits against the indifference of natural forces: of balancing on a hairline; yet I felt confident that if the straining little engine failed at this low altitude she could be put down almost anywhere in safety because of the light wing loading.

Even in the first gently banked turn, to keep within the confines of the airfield, I could tell how naturally she flew: light, firm, stable—giving precise response to touch dictated by my sub-consciously calculating instincts through a telegraph of reflexes undiminished in speed despite lack of continuous air practice. She was game! Whatever might befall, we would manage.

The scarlet wings swept round with growing confidence above the quiet earth. Slowly the horizon widened second by second as we climbed, revealing vistas of field and tree glowing in the last flood of evening light. A new eagerness awakened as though I walked hurrying to catch the spirit of my youth, for the far horizons beckoned no whit differently from old, luminous with promise, luring me on even though I could guess well enough the broad outline of what lay beyond. Life is one's personal past, com-pounded with the ticker-tape instant of the present, endlessly stimulated with renewed and different expectation. I had seen and experienced. There had been longing and reality; adventure as well as imprisonment; those who had gone and those who had been true; quest; disillusion; fulfilment. Dream and fantasy and aspiration had drifted far into the ocean of time—yet though they had vanished over the rim of the world, the endless waters of the earth that saw their passage remained unchanged. The years had given deeper peace, as well as fuller knowledge of myself and other men.

Whirling propeller and clattering engine engulfed my thoughts in cavernous walls of sound that quickly became so great an imprisonment that all seemed silence. *Airymouse* flew sedately on, slowly climbing higher. Presently we reached 2,000 feet. The ice-smooth air stung rushing past, pressing like a frozen mask upon face and tightened lips. I had forgotten, in the comfort of modern enclosures and cabins, how bitterly cold an open cockpit can be in winter. With old-time aeroplanes we wore long leather coats and fleecy knee-boots, but I was using only a light raincoat—and there was a strong draught down my back.

Remembering the powerful metal wings that used to carry me at great speeds and heights, I looked speculatively at the pair of ten foot fabric-covered biplane twins each side of me. Very small they were to dare the empty depths of heaven. By comparison, flying those metal fighters and transports was more akin to captaining a cross-Channel ship than this sensitive little dinghy I now was sailing. Nevertheless, *Airymouse* was immensely strong, with bar-tight pairs of flying wires slanting to the fuselage from the top of each white interplane strut, and crossed by single landing wires. She possessed reserves of strength considerably greater than any current ultra-light monoplane, and had been stressed for aero-batics. Maybe one day I would venture to loop and roll her, and see if the old thrill of making such exaggerated manoeuvres could be regained. Or perhaps I would teach her to dance in the manner that my parasol *Widgeon* did in the long ago: smooth the rudder on, and as she swings, cross the aileron control in the opposite direction to hold the skidding; then slide her reciprocally with rudder and aileron the other way. Like a Viennese waltzer from more courtly decades she would chassé from left to right and right to left, swaying and bowing. But not today. This was a cautious return, flying in a smooth sea of air, through which I peered down translucent depths at a remote, still world of dwarfed fields and little trees and play-box houses.

I pressed *Airymouse* into another broad turn, her buoyant wings canting to the slight pressure of my fingers while her nose swept steadily sideways around the guide-rail rim of the horizon. That was how we were taught in earlier days: no blind flying instru-ments to be observed minutely—just a steady reading on the A.S.I., and at the most a bubble juggled to keep central in its inverted arc of glass, augmenting the tell-tale shift of slipstream on our faces.

Slowly the shadowed world spun beneath the brilliant scarlet of the lower wing. Our altitude had lifted the setting sun half above the earth again, until he glinted on far distances with

19

renewed clarity, leaving everything immediately below covered with darkening gauze. Steadily *Airymouse* turned through the soft and secret upper light. Southward I could see the burnished silver of the Solent, and beyond those waters the high hills of the Isle of Wight still bathed in brilliance. As we nosed further round, the slowly wheeling scene mistily revealed the distant loom of Sussex heights already dim and drowsing in the eastern dusk. With cautious apprehension I glanced more steeply down the darkening depths, and knew that soon we must descend or night would catch us out. At the most there were twenty minutes.

Straightening on a northward course for the now invisible air-field, and guided unthinkingly yet surely by the shadowed masses of the land, I stared far to the west as we flew. The last of day was vanishing at a thousand miles an hour, dropping over the earth's rim like a rocket streaming a flame of golden wake that would briefly illuminate village after village, town after town, and hill and wood and fields, and presently leave them in the same darkness that was already groping towards me. Were I flying a supersonic fighter I could keep up with day, watching the last reflection glitter across the seas, and follow it from shore to shore and continent to continent around the world. But in the opposite direction, city after city must be brilliant with artificial lights that night would presently extinguish one by one as she raced onward to catch the glow of yesterday, trailing the new dawn behind her. Already the lamps of the city below me were beginning to shine with double rows of opalescence where streets partitioned mass after mass of irregular dusky buildings. Westward, the last of the sun's rim vanished, and its golden wash was fading like a dying dolphin's colours.

Time to go back. A must. Cold calculation urged my trigger-happy senses that there was no need to panic. Night would not yet close and make me lost, even though already thickening below my wings. The myriad pin-point lamps would guide me, and there was time enough for easy landing in the dusk. But first I would briefly check performance.

I levelled off, and let *Airymouse* gain speed. The gale whipped even colder, slapping icily at my face. As the invisible pressure on the wings changed, the front truss wires slackened a little and began to vibrate to the swifter turn of engine. After three minutes the little aeroplane had attained her maximum speed. Flailing propeller and minute 38 h.p. could drive her no more than 65 m.p.h.—which implied 60 m.p.h. at the most when cruising. This was indeed a return to old time flight! Hastily I throttled the straining, rough little engine, feeling that if it vibrated much more it would burst. As we slanted steeply earthwards, the wind played on the twenty exposed structural and control wires, whistling wildly and humming deeper notes that filled the quiet sky with overtones. Down, down we dropped towards mankind's multitude tramping self-engrossed among the illuminated city streets, uncaring and unconscious that a little aeroplane was flying moth-like through their dusk. In the emptiness we were a mere drift of our own thought: a nothingness: we were dust, and to the dust must presently return.

I shifted a little uneasily in the hard seat. *Airymouse* stirred with awakened animation, fractionally dipping and lifting at the slight movement of my hand on the stick. She was very responsive. I rocked the control more deliberately. . . . Suddenly I became convinced that one last critical test, both of her and myself, must be made. With a whirr the engine fanned into power while the nose was held down. I pushed it steeper. The wires began to shriek. Tension mounted, and the whole structure strained with new determination. The moment the A.S.I. needle touched 85 m.p.h. I steadily pulled back the control, proportioning the rate to the reducing pressure on the elevators as they forced the nose up and up as speed fell off. Earth vanished: the propeller fanned against the empty blue. Idiot! Idiot! Why did you do it? Too late. We are upside down. Centrifugal pressure holds me tight in the seat. Craning my head backwards I searched for the ground, and with relief tinged by exultation, watch it come arching up towards my inverted wings. As we plunged over the top of the loop the city lights became far flung strings and pools of sparkling jewels—white, gold, green and red. Somewhere beyond lay the aerodrome, and as we swept from vertical I saw it momentarily framed in the dark whirl of the propeller. Without further control movement, except to throttle the engine, *Airymouse* dropped into her natural steep glide and headed home with happy confidence. Good little aeroplane, I thought. Stupid old man to throw a loop! But I felt twenty years younger.

The wires hummed a gentler note, as though regretting departure from the heights. A last light lingered in the sky, though all the land was shadowed blue and grey. In dropping curves, pleasurably inappropriate for the regulated level approach path required these days, I steered towards the aerodrome, radioless and undistracted by the incessant talk that fills the skies today. As master of my fate, and maybe that of others, I kept a constant look-out for aerial traffic. All I found were rooks and gulls returning to their night haunt, flying with patient, steady wing-beat, and very clear to see at my slow speed. They were un-disturbed by my proximity, but gave a perceptive glance. Another augury, I thought. When warm weather comes we will fly with the birds as we did of old in my earlier slow-flying aeroplanes. In those days nobody had made close study of birds from the air, but for twenty years I was fortunate in having many such oppor-tunities—the runs back to base after test flights, longer journeys north or east delivering aeroplanes, and especially many pleasure flights with light aeroplanes and sailplanes. I from my aeroplane, and a bird on the wing, might both look down and see without conscious thought, the identical, primitive earth that gave us shelter and food. Presently I began to understand that it is we who belong to the earth; not the earth to us. One looked down and saw, spread like an ecologist's map, the picture of cause and effect on landscape and beast, overwritten and etched with the history of man.

But not tonight, as *Airymouse* slid smoothly down the icy air. Already the far view had vanished with lower altitude. Quickly we dropped to a couple of hundred feet above the boundary hedge, gauging the glide to give ample height for a precise touch-down near the neon-lit hangar door. With growing hugeness every second, the dun-coloured aerodrome lifted and widened until it extinguished the dominance of the sky. Tufts of grass became distinct as I rounded off descent, slowly lifting the nose in order to turn surplus speed into level flight that skimmed the ground. For a dozen yards *Airymouse* floated, while I held off to the last of her buoyancy. As she finally sank, a slight backward touch on the control sent her rustling to the ground in an easy three-pointer. I had forgotten how gratifying the simple pleasure of finding one's judgement of timing and speed to be true.

'All right?' they asked when I had taxied in.

'Amusing,' I replied with as much nonchalance as possible.

They would never believe that this meant: 'Amazing, amazing!'—nor that my heart was filled with elation because those little wings had lifted me from imprisonment, and henceforth would offer the skies whenever I had an hour of freedom. Yet, as I climbed from the little machine, feeling carefully with my foot for the fragile wing, I recollected that these men around me were pilots too, and that all of us were united by a common bond that was inexpressible yet which each of us understood.

3 Lords of the Air

For long grey weeks winter had breathed coldly on naked hedge-row and frost-smoothed plough, making brittle the tired grasses of the fields. Presently there came a period of rest. The countryside seemed waiting, as though in the awakening silence before dawn. Then suddenly everything changed. The sun, hidden these many days, shone from a cloudless sky. The earth stirred, restless with uprising life.

There had been no opportunity of collecting my new acquisition. *Airymouse* had been languishing these several months, neglected and increasingly dusty, in a corner of the big hangar which had seen her construction. Perhaps she thought that I had turned her down after all too brief acquaintance. But when Spring came tiptoeing into the consciousness of the countryside, freshening the skies with fragile blue, unrest stirred in man as well as her.

Tommy of war-time Spitfire days, with his invariable reliability, leapt to the breach and flew *Airymouse* to me.

'Quite a ride, Squire,' he said with an amused grin as he eased out of the cockpit. 'Stood stock-still in every gust. Average ground speed 40 m.p.h. Splendid vibro-massage! Otherwise O.K.'

All next morning it was difficult to work. Every window framed the blue highway of escape. The far horizons beckoned, and all the air was full of song. Out there was the world of freedom which once had seemed my own. I stared through the glass at unfettered skies, remembering the spaciousness and peace. To sit here became unbearable. In the sunshine of the mid-day break I went to the aerodrome, where *Airymouse* waited. Somewhere in the blue, larks were singing, and circling rooks cawed as they tumbled jubilantly above the boundary elms. Eagerly I climbed into the cockpit, buckled the lap strap and went through the routine of starting.

When the engine was warm and tested I waved away the chocks, and my little aeroplane ran swiftly to the farther hedge where she turned to face the drift of wind. I opened the throttle. She ran forward, wheels pattering with increasing lightness as wings took the weight, until with a last tentative bound she flung herself into her element. The fringe of elms slipped under wing, and the fair familiar vista that had been mine so many years spread once again.

There was a glory in the air—a flow of light that glowed upon the earth and bathed it with soft gold. On hedge and treetop, bronze twigs and branches were tipped with buds that glistened in a hundred shades of madder, swelling with readiness to unfold quietly breathing leaves and pollened blossom. Sallows and willows were clumps of scarlet, and larch trees made a tawny flame. Even the black tracery of oaks was invested with velvet sheen, and their long springtime shadows lay like calm dark pools among the bright green grass.

Airymouse canted in a gently banking turn whilst I watched the slowly spinning world unfold new scenes. The looming Quantocks in the middle distance slid away and the Blackdown Hills replaced them, presently yielding smooth Dorset Heights as the nose swung east of south. I straightened and flew onwards, reaching towards the far sparkle of the sea. My wings pressed smoothly on the rushing air.

I glanced at the gilt hands of a clock on a passing church tower. For thirty minutes I could dream that the skies were mine and that time stretched endlessly ahead. There, spread far and wide below me, was England, more gently beautiful than any of the other lands I knew. From my slight height in the skies above her I saw the loveliness of rounded hills, and at their feet the little fields, sunlit and serene within brightly outlined boundary hedges set like the tumbled meshes of a net tossed across the vales.

I swung *Airymouse* into a steeply tilted curve, feeling the wings press harder against the air. Still turning, I lifted her in a slow spiral another thousand feet. The countryside spun sedately like a many-coloured wheel while I looked outwards towards the rim.

The humped hills changed in slow procession from those of Dorset to Hampshire, Wiltshire and Somerset, until yet again the steep wall of the Dorset downland loomed before me, its plateau etched far as eye could see with habitation shadow marks of primitive men who long ago lived and died unrecorded except for those earthly signs. Of them the smooth turfed hollows and flattened banks spoke more significantly than all the regimented tree-fringed fields of later men. My gaze encompassed two thousand square miles of countryside and saw the history of its many years painted like a picture book.

Time caught my thought. I estimated there should still be fifteen minutes before I need return to the office. Subconsciously I banked the little aeroplane towards my home much as I used to at the end of each flight; but as the nose swept round, two sky specks came in view and, quickly drawing nearer, materialized into twin buzzards soaring on steep dihedral wings. Curving the circle wider to encompass them, I looked along my topmost wing and saw the birds like giant butterflies, motionless side by side, their wide-opened pinions bowed upwards in the wind.

Even as I watched, their calm flight turned to play. One drew in its wings and, closing the tips to points, plunged headlong towards a copse crowning a short ridge. Like an anchor descending through clear water, the steeply tilted buzzard plummeted towards the foreshortened trees. In ten seconds it became a golden dot barely discernible—so far had it fallen—but suddenly the great wings shot out and the bird soared majestically upward and upward, powerfully breasting the wind. The tremendous impetus carried it to a station nearly as high as its companion. For a few moments both stayed soaring, separated vertically by a hundred feet—then the top one unexpectedly hunched its wings, and nosing over deliberately dived at the other with an exuberant intentness that nevertheless seemed to be in play. Maybe its plunge was a mere two seconds, but at the very instant that impact looked certain the lower bird flicked on its back, fiercely extending intimidating yellow claws. Nonchantly the other swept past, only to recover in a graceful upward curve. Instantly its inverted companion rolled wing over wing upright and in a smooth quick diving movement rushed into the chase.

From black silhouettes they changed to glinting bronze as the sun altered in relation to my circling aeroplane. In the crystal clear air every movement of wings and tail and head was visible as they soared and tumbled, rolled over, and swept up again—sometimes chasing each other, sometimes in wingtip formation. The wild cries they wailed excitedly upon the skies were lost in the staccato rumble and racket of my own circling wings.

Suddenly mutually tiring of their play, both slanted down on a determined steady path, keeping within two wingspans of each other as they raced towards the leafless wood. From my altitude, a thousand feet above, it looked as though nothing could prevent them smashing into the trees. But miraculously the steep path changed into level flight, and on broad brown wings they skimmed the brightly budding twigs, sailing far across the wood, only to vanish as they landed among the screening branches of a tree.

Three weeks later I was reminded of them. No aerial meeting this time, for I was sitting in the warm spring sunlight that poured upon my cottage terrace. The earth had fully awakened. The song of countless birds mingled and filled the air as I lay back staring with unseen eyes into the deep blue of the zenith. Drowsily I became aware that from the heights came distance-muted mewling cries.

Lazily I groped for the binoculars. Into focus came the un-mistakable, great emarginated wings of two buzzards soaring with scarcely any forward movement. The wild, mournful insistence of their calls fell slowly towards me like scattered, drift-ing leaves. Side by side the two hawks were spiralling steadily upward, the male a little above, as though dominating his mate. Three or four thousand feet high, they presently reached the limit of rising air. Into swifter circles, horizontal now, they swung with a fiercer but effortless intensity, as though fired with the joy of life. There was a majestic freedom in their glide through sunlit space. Yet always the female remained a little below, matching with the precision of a dancer her companion's rhythm of movement.

Without warning, in a lightning-swift flick of pinions, the lower buzzard rolled on her back, floating with wings extended. At almost the same instant her companion lifted his wings so high above him that the tips were all but touching—then dropped like a parachute, long legs dangling. Claw reached for claw as the birds touched and closed on each other, breast to breast. Tight in each other's grasp, the female still on her back, each held wings wide outspread as they sank towards the distant earth in a long vertical stalled descent.

Through the glasses I could see the stillness of their drop, the strange biplane aspect of their superimposed wings steady against the wind, tilted bodies clutched together, heads beak to beak a little way apart. Down they sank, steadily under perfect control, dropping no faster than a feather. Maybe they fell for two minutes, floating gently towards the earth, as though sublimely unaware of it. Knowing they must be getting close to the ground I stole a glance from the binoculars and saw that the birds now were scarcely two hundred feet above the coppice on the low hill in front of me. Undistracted they continued drifting down. The topmost twigs were in the glasses. Still pressed together the buzzards passed below tree-top level a few yards in front of the wood, and in that instant broke apart, the female rolling off her back so quickly that she was but a yard behind her companion as they swung right-handed over the valley. With a quick moth-like flutter of wings they lifted, only to hold pinions still and fully extended. The breeze blowing up the slope caught them, and the buzzards floated slowly above the trees. Soaring yet higher they swung ponderously round and drifted silently across the wood. A sudden chatter of birds closed round them as they vanished.

Some weeks later I had occasion to walk those woods. There was a subdued note of sadness in the great spring chorus of the evening birds. The earth had found fulfilment. Even the air was relaxed and still. Among the tranquil aisles of trees the limpid level light was glowing, illuminating with new brilliance each trunk and branch and leaf. Far across the distant water-moorlands the sun was sinking towards the purple Mendip Hills.

So often, high above those hundred thousand Wessex fields my wings had soared, as though in emulation of countless generations of birds who had possessed this sky view a million years before man learned to fly. Wing after wing had sung its way across these heavens. What if the years had slowly changed this land? Always there was the spring; always high summer declining to autumn, stirring anew through winter, and bursting into fresh life with springtime again.

And then I saw them. Where the bluebells soon would shimmer, a great brown wing projected stiffly twisted among the pale green stalks. The evening sky grew colder. Ten paces further another blood-stained feathered bundle was spread-eagled, half hidden in the grass. Only a little way across that woodland space were two more buzzards side by side, their tumbled broad bronze moth-wings awkwardly crumpled around lifelessly drooping heads, and their great hooked beaks a little open, as though at the moment when gunshot racked them each had called the other in a wailing echo to the emptying skies.

4 Ride of the Valkyries

It was a day that dawned with eager expectancy and began to speed through the hours with the excitement of a long-legged colt discovering the first delight of hooves a-flying. The air possessed a compelling freshness, a pagan instability and thrill. Morning raced across the awakening world as though with certain knowledge that new happiness would be discovered in the next minute or a minute more ahead. But I was waiting—waiting for Andy to finish tuning the little two-cylinder engine.

An hour passed, and still I waited. In that time a subtle alchemy began to stir, brushing a hundred diaphanously steamy puffs across the blue. Sprung from the sun's radiance, those wraiths of moisture were the peaks of powerfully rising air, lifting like bubbles to condense into cloud when dew point was reached. With the magic of metabolism, they formed one after another, until the first hundred became a thousand presaging a thousand more, which presently dappled the sky from horizon to horizon. Even as I studied them, they expanded full and gleaming, drifting on a placid tide that slowly bore them north.

Andy glanced at his watch. 'Afraid it'll be another half-hour,' he said.

'Too bad,' I vaguely echoed, gazing at the gleaming beauties sailing across the blue.

But Andy was staring across his shoulder. 'Look at that!' he exclaimed.

Low over the hill beyond the town a red sailplane with silver wings was circling, fighting for height. It was a losing battle. The long open area of grass airfield was tempting as it offered easy access for the retrieving crew, so in a long flat curve the machine slowly slid towards it. Mid-span air brakes shot out. Decisively the nose tilted steeper, and with nice judgment the pilot came skimming in and landed on the grass strip behind *Airymouse*. Scarcely had he tipped to a stop than I again happened to glance towards the hilltop. High above it, three more sailplanes were circling. Round and round, steadily they rose, and after a few minutes sailed away westward. Beautiful as ribbon-winged albatrosses they soared across the blue, competing for distance. The pilot of the red sailplane ruefully watched them diminish and pass out of sight.

'Hard luck,' I commiserated.

He grinned. 'You need only make a single mistake and you're out of it—but I made plenty!' And he walked towards the Control Tower to telephone his whereabouts.

Lazily I lay back, and closed my eyes. In imagination I soared the sky in the manner that so enraptured me long ago—the wings of my sailplane inclined at gentle angle against the pressure of the air, buoyed up by the widespread upward movement of the atmosphere. Though instruments are essential to interpret a thermal current and aid exploration of its bounds, man can sense, with something of a bird's ability, whether he is flying in an area of air which is soarable. Instead of the ice-smooth downward slide that gravity gives, a light initial tugging may be felt, as though the sailplane is riding swiftly over slippery cobble-stones. Then comes a steady surge like the upward rush of a lift. In strong thermals even the rasping of the slipstream seems to alter key, possibly because the pressure change due to increasing height acts swifter than the automatic compensation of one's ears. The green pip of the variometer leaps upward. Quicker than conscious thought fingers press the stick to cant the wings, and with slight foot movement the sailplane is ruddered into circle after circle to keep within the invisibly rising air. Gradually the endless spirals drift downwind, and the earth drops away with almost imperceptibly increasing remoteness. Flight feels serene and safe as sailing on a mill-pool. Yet presently lift weakens. The sailplane is straightened, and gracefully moves onward, whispering across the heights, while its pilot scans sun-warmed fields and sky clouds for potential source of further lift—calculating, rejecting, accepting. But there is beauty to occupy him too: vast vistas of countryside and cloudscape re-newing assurance that the ancient laws of life are eternal and inescapable, bleak though the future of the dawning age may seem to men on earth. . . .

I stirred from my dream. My hands touched the living turf. I felt the crisp coolness of each green blade. The sun was warm upon my face. Surely I merely imagined that the world had problems? Sufficient to find the sky a magic blue, across which the bright clouds slowly sailed as though embarking on a voyage of discovery.

'Millions of thermals,' I called to Andy, 'wonder if I could soar with *Airymouse*?'

Though pundits talk of lapse rates in technical jargon that defines modulation of up-currents with the atmosphere's decrease in temperature as height grows greater, it does nothing to convey the physical impact of weather. What did it matter that those growing cumulus were children of a lapse rate where temperature had fallen a swift 6°F every thousand feet up, whereas when low overcast reigns the drop is a mere 1°F? In actuality the softness of the breeze was stirring with unrest that outweighed any hint of science. The great dome of the skies whispered and beckoned as though promising to reveal still greater secrets and even more magnificent adventure.

'Nearly ready,' said Andy.

Five minutes later I was at the controls. *Airymouse* rushed across the turf, pressing her wings against the heady, dynamic breeze. Swiftly she became buoyant, tugging at the bonds of earth more and more lightly as she felt promise of release, until with a last patter of wheels, movement blended into smooth lifting. On a long slant we began climbing towards the clouds. Five thousand hours of flying could not dull the wonder of the metamorphosis each time I flew. As though a miracle was taking place, I watched the lengthening panorama of trees and hedges frame more and more fields that grew smaller with remoteness every minute of increasing height. A great stillness takes possession of the earth, hiding the frenzied activities of men, and it almost seems the gods once more are singing from high places.

Across the sky to my left a thick blue bar of smoke was rising at a steep diagonal. My gaze following it downward found tongues of flame flickering from a mound of burning hedge trimmings. The smoke rose slowly writhing, sloped by the drift of wind, expanding and diffusing as it climbed, until at last it faded into haze darkening the flat base of one of the summer clouds slowly drifting above.

Now we'll see, I thought, and reduced power until just insufficient for *Airymouse* to hold height whilst flying at 40 m.p.h. Had I throttled fully we would have dropped 500 feet a minute; yet with power set as it was, the sensitive altimeter showed no greater rate of descent than a sailplane. So I flew half gliding towards the column of smoke. Its diameter, as we neared, was much larger than expected, and a pungent smell of burning wood permeated the air as *Airymouse* touched the fringe. One wing gave a slight kick as it entered the rising air. I began to circle, passing time after time from clear air to smoke. On each contact our slow descent was checked. A few more times and the climb indicator began a slight rise, gaining nearly two hundred feet in the next minute.

'There you are!,' I called to *Airymouse*. 'That's nearly as fast as you usually climb using full engine.'

She ignored me. Diligently round and round we went, slowly

sucked upward through the diagonal track of gradually diffusing smoke. Presently the cloud base was so near that I could perceive it had the texture of a broad undulating layer of steam. Twelve minutes had gone and the altimeter showed 2,800 feet. An instant later *Airymouse* left the smoke and was nosing into the towering blue-shadowed flank of the cloud. White vapour swirled dazzlingly around the windscreen, and then snatched the earth from sight. Dramatically, we were imprisoned, hemmed in with isolation that compressed my very life to an intensity of concentration on the suction driven gyro-horizon I had recently fitted. Only ghostly wingtips showed through the fog. Sense of movement vanished. Minutes became timeless, while I waited with abnegation for time to unroll and restore the shadow-dappled brilliance of the earth. The engine rattled louder. The walls of my prison grew tense with minute vibrations. The pointers of the flight instruments bored into my brain, defying with their indications the guesses of my senses at what the aeroplane was doing. With studied deliberation, I strove to keep a steady rate of turn and speed.

Whether we made one circle or three was beyond immediate power of deduction, for I was intent on holding perfect turns. Yet almost against my will I snatched a glance at the wings, and saw them reassuringly carved with icy immobility upon the opaque mist. That slight movement of my eyes resulted in all sense of orientation vanishing, and I imagined *Airymouse* was banking vertically. With nerve-taut swiftness I sought the turn indicator. My senses were circus creatures caged; controlled yet desiring to get out of the blinding imprisonment; rebellious but tamed by a conditioned mind which knew that this calculated, curving path would achieve in appropriate time a preconceived result. We had only to turn with steady equilibrium a little longer, and the machine inevitably must reach clear sky above—but through lack of practice the requisite delicate, three-dimensional juggling of controls was no longer instinctive. I could remember the same state of mind when discovering the art while pioneering some of the development of blindflying instruments nearly forty years earlier.

At this moment the wings rocked violently, and the dull

vapours puffed a glow of translucent white. With a surge we burst from the side of the cloud, stunned by the dazzling bright- ness of day. Orientation clicked back as the horizon flicked into position in my consciousness. I reset the wings to this datum. Still turning, I looked back at the blue-shadowed snow drift which had imprisoned us and saw that its bulging top towered at least another 500 feet higher. Could this effulgent monster really be one of those little scraps of cloud, which as a steamy puff of saturated thermal an hour earlier I could span with half a finger as I gazed at it from the ground? Equally our new relationship of exterior view denied that this rounded glowing beauty, sailing so serenely, was the formless, trackless whiteness where seconds ago we had lain dependent in instruments for balance, waiting for release. The sense of peril which my senses had so vividly conjured was swept into the easiness of imperfect recollection. In its place was the relief of escape, while everywhere about me great blue avenues of space led to beckoning new horizons. I opened up the engine.

Onward and upward we went, scaling the brilliant heavens. Flee from the trammels of earth, sang my thought. Soar into sun- filled freedom. Empty the mind. Float in the serenity of nothing- ness! And *Airymouse* lifted ever higher, pressing the silk buoyancy of air with sensitive wings. The skies thundered the music of our freedom as I swung the aeroplane with smooth trajectory across the soaring Cyclops eye of the sun, the starboard planes raised high in the sky momentarily shielding my own eyes from its blinding dominance. The limpid pressure of the air was trans- mitted, through the lightly upturned aileron to my finger tips as *Airymouse* reacted to the slight control movement returning her wings level.

No sweep of brush could paint a curve more perfect than that turn, for flying has the ritual rhythm of a ballet in the air: a harmony of motion as though living the very curves with which nature draws the clouds. . . . And the turn completed I looked up again at the vapour peak which was my goal. For a moment I stared incredulously. Down the long avenue of blue a glitter of many insects caught my eye.

35

Round and round they circled, their burnished wings reflecting the sun. Quickly they came into sharper focus, and I saw some were bright with scarlet, others bronze or blue; some were multi-coloured; one was white. I craned my head into the buffeting slipstream, lifted my goggles and stared.

Through those long clear vistas between the endless rows of widely separated cloud, I could see Wessex as though it was a vast pastel bowl, rimmed by glittering seas and far hills. In the great dome of blue surmounting it flashed and faded and flashed again, among clouds dappling the middle distance, the iridescent wings and bodies of what I could now see was a multitude of sailplanes rising in a column bright as a barber's pole. Six, eight, ten, a dozen I counted throwing circle after circle. I had forgotten that sailplanes were using my home skies. Though five miles distant, I was at the same level as the lowest, with the topmost a thousand feet higher. Opening the throttle wide I headed *Airymouse* towards them, climbing at her best. As we rose slowly higher the clouds in their remoteness became a hundred thousand cloudlets strewn like regimented petals across the far green fields.

Slowly we drew across the countryside, but the sailplanes were outclimbing the aeroplane. Even the lowest was now a thousand feet above our level. Intent as their pilots must be in watching against collision as they circled round and round, it was unlikely that they had even seen my stubby scarlet wings. Higher and higher the sailplanes went, exploiting the thermal to the limit of its lift—long-winged and beautiful, their flight the most graceful perfection of a pilot's art. It is the only true flying—the soaring of a bird.

While I was still someway distant, the topmost sailplane straightened and sailed off westward. A scarlet machine followed, and then the white one with gold wings. The others continued steadily circling upward from their lower altitudes. Turning *Airymouse* I scanned the wide horizon, peering into the entrancing distance as though it was a crystal gazer's ball. When I looked back, every sailplane had vanished.

Lingering in the sunlit solitude, I speculated on the impulse urging men to take to the air and find such pleasure in these vast vistas. It is a god-like aspiration and fulfilment. Flying remote and high, the deep quiet of a peace unfindable on an earth where torment, anger, and darkness so readily rule, becomes a way of revelation. There is escape; fulfilment; life's inextinguishable dream of the ideal; the majesty of power and space—but what does it matter why we flew? Sufficient that today had special beauty, where cumulus opened like tropic flowers, swiftly swelling their steamy filaments into fantasies of towering white. Tall tips, still slowly climbing, unrolled like frosty fronds. I stared at the rows of turbulent beauties sprung from tattered elfins born of the sun warmed earth—and found that their towering proximity had turned my aeroplane into a presumptious gnat hovering over their tops. Though I could force myself to believe that I had watched these giant cumulus grow from an unclouded morning sky, it no longer seemed possible that each had been merely a heated bubble cooling as it rose; losing capacity to hold moisture and slowly condensing to cloud; rising and expanding in steadily rarifying air and releasing its heat of condensation to maintain temperature anew; rising with fresh impetus and condensing still more until it became the majestic cloud I saw, a mile wide and equally as tall.

Tremendous instability, I muttered to myself. Instability? Latent heat? Thermodynamics? Did such words explain the wonder of the clouds? They could lift and drop and viciously tilt a ten ton aeroplane as though it was a dinghy riding perilous over-falls. Flying through the monsoons of India I had seen clouds tower higher than Everest, terrible in their might—or in their strata form, more treacherous than the mightiest desert. Time after time with war-time fighters I had burst through barriers of cloud to find in the wine-dark heights a loneliness that was absolute, my wings sealed from mankind by an unending floor of white-ness. At others, vast echoing cloud valleys had lain beneath a higher canopy, and I had flown their long avenues walled with whiteness on either hand, half horrified yet impelled by the very mystery of cleft and gorge to fly further and explore, despite the air of malignity and dark, brooding threats. Such clouds are the very antithesis of the magnificent creations of high summer, where cumulus may float like towering mountain islands ten miles long, with glittering pinnacles and blue buttressed mysteries inviting happier and more exuberant exploration. Carefree as swift or swallow, with soaring zoom and whirling bank I would wheel across the filmy boundaries, and plunge down steep valleys, leap a headland, drift obliquely through mauve-shadowed, golden chasms, where blue caves gleamed—only to lift up and up in one tremendous, soaring climb, back to the beckoning sky through portals where castellated domes crown the many columned snow-palaces of my adventuring.

On other days a tired, drab world has lain shadowed beneath weeping clouds. Perhaps far away a shaft of light has drawn me, so that I have winged upwards through its beam to where the same blue sky beckons as though it was a radiant window in the darkness. At full power, my fighter of old would thrust its snarling way between encircling cloud banks, until at last its wings brushed through the final writhing frill of topmost vapour and into the dazzling sky-space of the sun. In the crystal silence I have circled, awed as a pilgrim who at last has achieved the shrine, until diminishing fuel has hurried me back to the hole in the cloud, there to plunge into its black well, hurtling with screaming wings down the long path I climbed so hopefully a little while before. As though it is a dark corridor of transition, that dive presently leads into a different life, flying in the dull light between two levels of cloud—and there, beyond the edge of the lower layer, at last spreads the dim olive texture of the familiar earth.

I may not like blind flying, but the clouds are tamed at last. They can arch unbroken across the world, thousand upon thousand miles, yet cause no hindrance to the captain of an air-liner trained to trust electronic guidance by gyro, radar and radio. For me it is enough to emulate the birds. They never fly in cloud, and only through mist when the ground is discernible as a balanc-ing datum. I am a fair-weather pilot in these older years, content to watch earth and sky in all their changing manifestations of sunlit beauty. But there is more. Man's heart is uplifted at possessing the freedom of a bird; there is nobility in high solitude and vast expanse; there is wonder at the imposing design of nature, and in perceiving the long extent of human struggle to win a place. Flight is an allurement as well as a challenge, whose acceptance brings spiritual fulfilment complimentary to music, the charm of women, and the sweetness of home.

So with wires singing, *Airymouse* came down at last from the clouds, sighing back to the turf of her home. Repose enfolded me like quiet song. For a last few minutes we skimmed the grasses reluctant to leave the skies, then the wheels lightly touched the ground and *Airymouse* rolled to a stop by her hangar. For a moment I watched the clouds majestically sailing an intense blue sky, in which flashed wings of even deeper blue—and I realized that all the air was filled with the sweet twitter of hunting swallows.

5 Render no Song

In a summer sky so cloudless and devoid of haze that the earth stretched into boundless distance, *Airymouse* was humming quietly above the great ploughed fields into which the upland Downs had been converted, since the last war, by tractors capable of rendering the farthest field only a few minutes from the farm-stead. But I remembered all this area of my boyhood as a boundless rolling sea of fragrant turf starry with flowers, its silence emphasized by the song of countless skylarks. In those days these Downs were grazed by endless flocks of sheep—just as they had been for 600 years. Of the old, unspoilt quiet the only recognizable reminders are the broad droves along which sheep were once herded, and the high ridgeway of the steep northern bluff. Yet as *Airymouse* lifted buoyantly across the grassy banks of Uffington Castle, above the ancient White Horse carved in the chalk, a vista opened in the vale beneath that was as familiar and unchanged as though I left it yesterday instead of a lifetime ago. Bathed by brilliant sunlight, it basked in drowsy stillness, yet hinted a consciousness which

knew that this was yet one more June of a countless succession
back to the world's beginning.

Through the whistling air I dived towards the hidden distance
where the Thames was winding through summer haunted
meadows below the Cotswold Hills. My wings slid smoothly as
a scarlet palette knife across a newly painted canvas of elegiac calm,
and in ten minutes discovered the river deep and green beneath
cool willows. As I turned to follow its course, a kingfisher in a
streak of blue fire darted from the reedy bank and sped downstream, and when I dropped lower the bulrushes swayed as a
moorhen scuttered into flight, dabbling whorles of water. Nothing
had changed. I remembered youthful summers: the soft lap and
rustle of the current; the gold fields of buttercups and great white
dog daisies; tall comfrey, and water betony, purple loosestrife,
wild mignonette, sunflower gold of ragwort and spiked agrimony;
the freshness, the heedless delight of an unfolding world. . . .
Staring down I saw it all again.

Beneath my wings and into my awareness, tugging at recollection and abruptly becoming real, appeared a particular riverside
field that I had long forgotten. It was exceptionally big but
relatively narrow. As the mists of time rolled clear I remembered
a slow and stately Maurice Farman 'Shorthorn' of the First World
War—its pusher Renault engine erratically misfiring as it headed
towards this spot.

At the sound I had scrambled from my boat in the lock nearby
to discover in the distance this white biplane of enormous dimen-
sions flying low across the river. When over the far end of the
meadow, the nose suddenly dipped so steeply that the spidery tail
booms and their rudders showed clearly above the top wing. With
a bump the twin pairs of skid mounted wheels touched the turf,
and in a succession of diminishing bounds the machine came
running tail-high down the field. I raced to where it stopped, its
glistening walnut propeller still whirling slowly—the engine
going *rumpity-rumpity-bang*. The engine stopped. Two leather-
coated, goggled men climbed from the stubby, grey nacelle
perched high in the cat's-cradle of varnished spruce struts and

thin bracing wires. I gazed breathlessly at these gods whom I longed to emulate. Presently they changed a sparking plug or two, and flew away. The translucent, long wings, rocking in the sunlight, slowly receded with the power and majesty of the Thames' own swans.

Airymouse gave a similar protesting heave as I turned her from the cool air of the river in order to circle the field. I made a long leg to the end where the legendary Farman came down. The turf stretched unhampered and level, with length enough to land and take off my own small machine a dozen times in succession. Yet it would not be my wheel marks that made history — but the six glimmering lines of ghostly bent grass where the four main wheels and scraping tail-skids of the phantom *Rumpity* still romantically lingered in my mind's imagination. As I straightened up and again began to follow the river downstream, I remembered how that old-time biplane headed diagonally away, and now realized that I knew without doubt to which little aerodrome it had gone that far away day. I would fly there in a moment and find its relic. It had been the Mecca of my schooldays.

The foothills drew closer to the river, growing rich and comfortable with shaded lawns and gracious houses shielding behind a fringe of chestnuts, acacias and elms. Here was a remembered islet, a familiar backwater, a weir, and a drowsy little town whose time-tinted houses each side of the river were linked by a long wooden bridge. At its side was the legendary Inn, still almost unchanged, set in a rose garden by the edge of the water where in my schooldays we used to have tea after a long row up the river.

For a fleeting instant I glimpsed the timelessness of time, but in a flash *Airymouse* had carried me beyond the tumbling water of the nearby weir, and the river began a broad bend before taking a gap between the north and southern hills. At my port wingtip the Cotswolds lifted high, crowned with beech and oak where, as a boy, I tried to track with Indian silence a stray deer that sometimes might be revealed, still and tense, among the dappled leafy aisles. With light stampede it would melt into the shadows where red squirrels chattered, and gawdy jays, screaming harshly, fled undulating among the boughs, leaving only the wind whispering in the topmost leaves.

Throttled to slow speed so that I could watch more easily, *Airymouse* floated past unchanged meadows whose banks so often had seen us moored within our cape-cart hooded camping boat. In this reach of river I learned to row and swim and sail, and played the art of cooking with steaming billycan upon an open fire. Beyond it there drew close a place more important than all. On one side meadows flowed into the placid distance of the Berkshire vale: on the other steep wooded slopes filled the view—and then gave place to the hill, the great curved hill with the river at its feet, where a young mother and her small son used to play in the sunny spaciousness of days that vanished with the First World War. The hum and whistle of the wind in the wires was like a sigh as I remembered.

Abruptly *Airymouse* turned from the spell. In the middl. distance sprawled a city of industrial chimneys and serried suburbs. It had grown enormously since last I saw it, typifying the lateral spread of urban life when instead buildings should be climbing skyward to make fair gleaming cities where once stood slums. Yet, as we drew nearer, the soft foliage of many trees and the green spaces of turf in gardens gave it a more open setting than the starkly uprearing functionalism of modern buildings. In the clear light of this bright morning I began to recognize half a dozen open spaces on the outskirts linked with my re-awakening memory of early flying days.

Far away in 1911 there had been that glimpse of Cody, sitting stalwart and exposed in the battering slipstream of his slowly moving, pusher biplane, with its great distinctive elevator in front. I did not know then that he was making his prize-winning Michelin flight, but with fascination saw him swing the impressive machine ponderously round and follow another railway which presently took him to his base at Farnborough. From that moment my wooden building blocks were turned into aeroplanes having cardboard wings.

Next year we paid to see an oil-stained Blériot monoplane make cautious circuits from a wood-encircled field—which twelve months later saw young Hamel, and his dashing black Morane-Saulnier, thrilling everyone with startling turns and some of the earliest loops. Indeed, on this last occasion I took a big decision: gambled on six copies of the local penny paper offering free flights to lucky numbers—and lost my entire fortune of three weeks' savings. Nevertheless, it stirred determination to have my own aeroplane one day—not dreaming fulfilment must wait forty years. Today, a little late in life, I circled the scene of this ambition. Not far away I could see other spaces significant to me, but their secret unknown to other generations. Even at this moment my starboard wing was sweeping past a small Park where, one frosty Christmas early in the Great War, three Vickers pushers descended—two in safety; the other wrecked against a tree. A little beyond was the grass practice field of a riding school where four-horse artillery limber-carriages of early war years thundered round a clinker perimeter, and a slick little de Havilland monosoupapé pusher fighter had landed on the undulating central turf to stay a summer day while I gazed at it from every angle. Months later a slender B.E.2c. came drifting through the evening air and settled on that same field with the softness of a butterfly. A year or so afterwards I heard the rumbling rattle of a splendid khaki painted Bristol Fighter as it circuited and landed. While *Airymouse* completed her won circuit over that oasis among the houses, I looked ahead another mile, and found almost hidden among the trees a narrow sports ground where it seemed impossible that even those lightly loaded aeroplanes of old could land—yet they did! A scallop-winged Caudron first, bearing the unexpected red outer ring and blue centre of French insignia; months later came two Avro *504J's,* with rich smelling oil dripping from fabric wings and fuselage. Even the local gasworks produced the occasional thrill of a great netted balloon slowly inflating, and eventually ascending perilously among closely clustering gasholders, to drift away golden in the evening air.

These aerial creations seemed the quintessence of romance: not weapons of destruction, but dream inspired mechanical birds which I longed to be able to fly. Even to the youths who were my seniors in that Georgian generation, war was a romantic quest. They were knights in a cause, flocking in their thousand thousands, anxious to battle before it ended—and dying in their millions in vast, terrible, useless, long-draw gambles that gained or lost a mile or two of the devastated Flanders plain. To me war was an unreal stage, hidden beyond the guardian Channel seas. The whine of shells, the lethal ping of bullets, the earth-shaking thud of explosions, the mud, the rain, the misery, the zig-zag trenches, the ruins, endless flooded shell holes, were painted pictures, not the horror of reality. No meaning distilled from the tramp of feet, the converted buses and procession of primitive lorries, the blue-uniformed wounded hobbling slowly through the sunshine of those days. I stood in the path of history unaware of its dark, spasmodic progress; unable to appreciate that it subsisted on the stink of death, tearing away sons and lovers and sweeping suffering into the dust. Only as events receded with the years did there seem ordered sequence, like stepping-stones leading in an inevitable direction.

From *Airymouse* I gazed a lifetime back. The men who flew those war-time aeroplanes—the dark, the fair, the gay, the taciturn —were vanished, gone with the wind, as though their eager individualism had never been. Who remembered? Who still mourned? Yet even as I looked, it seemed that their striving and their hope, their dogged courage, their very lives, irradiated land and sky: intense, invisible, intangible; but giving solace and validity to all the slowly unfolding and inevitable stratagems of change and chance.

Changed and yet changeless, the pattern remains. Enswathed in the harsh rush of slipstream I could still see today and yesterday as we flew towards the edge of the city where the narrow Kennet makes a sudden sally from the open country, threading past rail-way yards and drably marshalled houses as it seeks the Thames. Just at the point I had imagined from recollection of long ago, there came in sight, beyond the ranked roof-ridges of a last sprawling factory, the diminutive war-time aerodrome, disused these two generations, where the Farman in 1916 had gone after its forced landing in that long, narrow field by the Thames over which I had flown twenty minutes ago. Unaltered, unbeautiful, but tugging at memory, the Farman's aerodrome lay between a right angle of the low river bank and a similarly angled line of elms. Even now I could see that it comprised two square fields which had been joined by filling their dividing ditch. On the slight ridge that was left, a lumbering F.E.2d., singing in from the hazy distance with sonorous *wong-awong*, had bounced and thunderously tipped on its nose. Down there, on the daisy fringed towpath, I had stood watching through many a school half-holiday. There it had all begun. One day I would be a pilot. . . .

Airymouse was canting round, helping me to scan the familiar field and gauge its roughness. Like the sports ground it seemed too small for all those war-time landings—yet almost before I was aware of my intention, we were in position leeward, slanting down with throttled engine, while ghosts of all the aeroplanes that landed there were plucking arpeggios of recollection on my humming bracing wires. A moment more, we were bumping across the tussocks—and long before the filled-in ditch, had stopped. *Airymouse* stood there with propeller ticking over, a little intimidated by the bigness that had suddenly materialized around her. As though spurring a horse, I turned her, and taxied to the corner nearest to the factory, where three T-shaped Bessoneaux canvas covered hangars once stood. I switched off; and climbed out, into the sunny silence.

The spirit of a small lad was with me. I saw him sitting by the river bank on just such a day as this—waiting: waiting through the morning and early afternoon. Occasionally he would stare into the weed-strewn depths of the turbid water, watching dimly gliding gudgeon and dace, or he might lie on his back and listen to almost invisible larks—but always his gaze returned to the half-revealing yet mysterious hangars gently billowing in an occasional puff of wind. The yellow, spearlike skid and shiny black nose of an Avro *504J* showed in the first; in the next stood a big Martinsyde *Elephant* with cowling removed, displaying the six polished

copper cylinders of an impressive 160 h.p. Beardmore; and the
last almost hid the most thrilling of all—a diminutive olive-
coloured Sopwith *Pup* with scarlet cowling encircling its 80 h.p.
Le Rhône rotary. The boy's thoughts lingered over the gleaming,
curved propellers; the subtle camber of those thin wings; the
slanting struts and multitude of wires. If only he was twenty
instead of thirteen!

That day it seemed there would be no flying. There rarely was.
Often he made the long journey to the aerodrome only to find the
aeroplanes in their hangars, or perhaps were pushed outside to
stand swaying lightly in the wind until late afternoon, when they
would be trundled in again. Just to be near these wonderful
creations was enough; somehow they seemed linked with the
invisible future, as though compelling arrows of silver were
showering to the far horizon. But this time there was more
practical activity. A field telephone buzzed. Mechanics in overalls,
wearing the jaunty R.F.C. cap, went from the last hangar to the
first. They ran out the Avro. There was hope! The mechanics
fussed around, making little adjustments. A fitter climbed in.
Chocks were kicked firmly under the wheels. A corporal tenta-
tively fingered the walnut blades. The elevators came hard up, and
two men leaned across the tail weighing it down. While the
propeller was being pulled over, the cylinders of the star-like
Gnome engine rotated with hollow noise, clanking and bubbling
their single big valves as each opened and shut.

'Contact!'

With a lusty swing, the engine fired and became a quadrant of
whirling silver where the black cowl was cut away at the bottom.
A cloud of pungently burnt castor oil billowed each time the
exhaust note rose and fell in obedience to the 'blipping' switch.
Soon the engine was spinning in a crescendo of din to its maximum 1,200 r.p.m., while the aeroplane strained and shuddered
at the chocks, and the grass behind the rudder shone brightly as it
bent pulsing to the slipstream. With a burst or two the roar died
and the propeller stopped.

A few minutes later a lean grey, open Mercédes stopped with a swirl of dust at the gate. An Ack-Emma rushed to open it. The car lurched in. At the wheel was the ace pilot of the local group, silk scarf flying in the wind. Here was the veteran of several hundred hours flying, survivor of a terrible crash; the hardened warrior; legendary hero of fantastic fights; the man who would rocket down the nearby city's main street just above the housetops and then zoom up and up. Here he was for a moment of hero worship: a slim, fair-faced youth, with almost feminine voice— and as he pulled on his tattered leather helmet one saw with sudden shock that he had only a single hand, for his left arm ended in a leather stump fitted with a neat silver-plated adjustable clamp.

He took a few quick puffs at a cigarette, then stamped it under heel before striding to the waiting Avro. The Sergeant-fitter sprang to attention and saluted. Giving careless yet friendly acknowledgment, the pilot placed a foot in the step-hole and swung himself astride the fairing, before sliding into the leather-rimmed rear cockpit. He buckled tight the wide webbing of his lap belt. There were no shoulder straps or parachutes in those simple days—nor radio. I saw him lean a little sideways and methodically clamp his maimed left arm to the fine-mixture lever of the rotary engine. Control surfaces wagged in turn. He nodded to the mechanic standing ready to swing the propeller.

'Contact!'

The engine stuttered into life, tensing the aeroplane with purpose. The chocks were pulled clear. Rocking on its narrow track, the white Avro picked its way across the meadow—and at the far and turned, poising like a dragonfly nerving itself for flight. Blue smoke trailed denser and streamed astern. The staccato purr forcefully intensified. Lightly the machine lifted its tail and began to move. In a hundred yards it took the air—the wire-spoked wheels still spinning as it climbed away. Higher and higher and further it droned into the blue. It vanished: but even as the boy got ready to go home, the sun flashed distantly on white wings as they turned.

This was a bonus day: the unexpected: the machine was coming back! It was a visible cruciform transparent in the blue: it had become an aeroplane distinct in outline. Louder swelled the mutter of the engine: it hummed high overhead. Those square wing-tips clearly identified the Avro design. It made a circuit and straightened.

Sudden silence descended from the heights. It was gliding: losing speed: slower and slower. Breathtakingly the nose lurched steeply down. Wings flicked; then flashed alternately. A spin— the most dangerous and advanced of all manoeuvres! Five turns, six, seven, eight: the aeroplane so low it was enormous as it flailed round, black nose hurtling towards the earth. Would it never pull out? A mere eight hundred feet to go. . . Was this going to be one of those terrible crashes one read about? . . . Abruptly the Avro stopped spinning. In a smooth confident curve the pilot recovered from the dive and came racing low across the aerodrome —only to sweep into a roaring zoom. Up: up: steeper and steeper: nose in the heavens, tail pointing to earth: leaning over backwards: upside down: vertical: steeply into level flight. Thrill of thrills and excitedly beating heart!

The engine faded into staccato moans as the aeroplane banked round, gracefully dropping towards the landing area. Skimming with steadily decreasing speed above the grass, the tail dropped lower— until, with a hollow thump and rumble, wheels and tail skid touched together, and using quick bursts of engine the biplane came swaying to the hangar. The propeller briefly speeded, then stopped. Silence. The lithe wings reverted to frail, canvas- covered structures: inanimate: the spirit of flight subdued.

For a moment the pilot sat unmoving, with the everyday world filtering back. He glanced at the men standing expectantly by the pile of red petrol cans with which they would laboriously refuel the machine. Unclipping his left arm from the throttle, he pulled off his helmet, cocked a leg over and jumped down the side of the fuselage. Slowly he walked round the wings to the shining black nose. Warm castor oil dripped from the bottom and was smeared on the sides. He paused and fondled a blade of the walnut propeller —then quickly bent and kissed the round edge of the cowling.

'Good-bye, old girl,' he said. 'That was a grand farewell flight.'

Abruptly he walked to the Mercédes, swung the crank, and with a crescendo of noise was gone.

Long after the bitterness of that war had faded, and the world was preparing for the next, a tall solidly built man of forty or more came one day to my office. His stance and appearance seemed vaguely familiar.

'My name is Jupp,' he said. 'I'm a schoolmaster, but I've come on the off-chance that you could use my services in lecturing at your flying school and doing the odd job of ferrying.'

'A lot of chaps come with the same hope,' I apologetically began. 'Trouble is, flying these days has become rather a different game, so the experience of the older crowd doesn't match modern requirements. Have you a commercial licence, for instance?'

'Fraid not. I'd get pipped by the medical for anything but a private licence,' and he waved a loose sleeve.

Where had I met him? That high voice! It suddenly dawned.

'A *504*, a *'Tinside*, and a *Pup!*' I said cryptically.

He looked at me keenly. 'How did you know?'

'I was one of the small boys who used to stand there for hours hoping that the "Mad Major" would fly.'

'Well, I'm damned,' he said—then added with gratified amusement: 'And did they really call me that?'

Not until the Battle of Britain was at its height did I encounter him again. He stepped from a Stinson with which he had ferried some pilots who were collecting a couple of Spitfires.

'Hello,' he said with a special grin. 'You see, I'm back on the job! Seen any Sopwith *Pups* recently?'

We met many times after that, but lost touch in the difficult post-war years. Then one day with sudden shock I read his obituary. Memory pictured him once more as the tall and slender 'Mad Major'—and I remembered all those others: those youthful millions who fought and died in the Great War they believed would be the end of all wars. . . . And there were all those in the next. . . . Across the space of time, like whispering leaves, I heard 'the dead returning, lightly dance.'

6 Blue Noon

Through tranquil skies I flew in peaceful oblivion of the engine's mutter, gazing at the sunlit countryside as though it was a fugue in time, with past and present for its theme. For an hour the pattern slowly unfolded, telling the story of uncounted years. Cattle browsed in level meadows where anciently a great river spread, and in adjacent higher ground, green wheat revealed faint marks of long forgotten Romans. Where medieval kings once hunted, the open forest had been converted through the centuries to field after field, in which the treeless turf disclosed bold scars where Neolithic man dug flint pits. On all sides the vanished years had left scattered signs and portents veiled lightly by the cultivation of today. Beneath it the earth's contours were scarcely changed from a million years ago: broad bosomed, lifting slow and lovely curves, with quiet valleys drowsing in the sun.

Intent though I was on a landscape that spread with ever changing interest far into the distance, a flash of reflected light caught my eye as lustred wings of darkest violet-blue crossed the line of vision. The summer fields were dismissed, for almost level with *Airymouse* two rooks soared on a bubble of rising air which the sun had drawn from the warm earth. They were exploiting a mechanism of the atmosphere that existed long before creatures evolved with power of flight, yet which man only recently learned to utilize with long-winged sailplanes riding from one up-current to the next.

In this buoyant playground the rooks cawed their pleasure as they circled the ambient sky, ignoring the muted mutter of my engine. Around them I drew a slow circle of wide radius from which I looked towards the imaginary centre and watched them soaring. Their spatulate, five feather fingertips were set in fan-like form to give greatest lift at the expense of a little extra resistance as they glided on stilled wings. On a lightly breezing day, when mild thermal currents rise from contrasting ground and crops, everyone has witnessed these birds circling slowly to and fro above the trees, while the upward moving atmosphere eliminates the inescapable descent that would occur in static air.

In flapping flight an artificial equivalent of the effect is obtained by the bird's forward motion due to the pull of gravity, compounded with increased lifting forces from the wings' downstroke. The trajectory of the rising and falling tips traces a long and shallow undulation through the air, giving crests, for a bird the size of a rook, which are some ten feet apart and less than one foot high. In cruising flight even the upstroke gives a little increment of lift, because the wing is raised at a small incidence superimposed on the shallow sine-wave of its motion. When rapid flapping takes place, such as for take-off and initial climb, the movement becomes largely a steeply twisted upward motion of the wing to get it in the shortest time to the raised position for the slower, vital down-stroke. To this end the tip feathers are relaxed, forming a series of little winglets which cut upward, like knives edgeways, at a steeper angle than obtainable by the maximum twist a bird can impose on the torsionally stiff wrist-joint from which these pinion feathers spring. On downstrokes of heavy impetus the tip feathers automatically spread, and because each curved shaft bends under air loads they assume individual angles of smaller incidence than the main wing. This avoids breaking down the hard worked air-flow by filtering it through the slots between the tip-feathers and increasing the lifting suction.

Viewed from ground level, wing motion seems merely up and down, but when flying above a bird it is clear that there is equally emphatic forward and backward movement. The action has counterpart in the instinctive forward thrust of one's arms to break a fall when feet stumble. A bird, launching from a branch, pushes its wings similarly outward and down, as though to press the air ahead and so lever itself horizontal instead of tumbling headlong. Indeed under every condition of flight it is the degree to which the wings are held slightly forward or aft of the centre of gravity that controls descent or climb.

Similarly, unsymmetrical positioning of each wing by retarding or advancing separately, rather than individual twist like ailerons, gives combined lateral and directional control, producing grace-fully curving flight path or quick turns. The tail is neither elevator nor rudder but a trimmer tilted in opposition to the upward or downward pitching effect of the wings, thus enabling the bird to hold at will any attitude the wing setting has moment-arily produced.

The pair of rooks I was watching suddenly ceased circling, and closed their wingtips to fine points giving the smallest resistance of all. Using the resulting flat glide they headed across the country-side, making no movement of their wings for many minutes. Like glowing black crosses they leaned in equipoise upon the smooth and sunny air while meadow after meadow slowly passed beneath. Straight as an arrow they flew. I followed a hundred yards astern, tacking like a ship to avoid overtaking. In a little while I saw, two miles ahead, a great field lying fallow, where yellow charlock had been ploughed in to clean the ground. Long before we got there, I could see that it was dotted with many rooks and jackdaws, so that I felt sure the destination of my couple was this red-brown, newly turned patch of earth.

For three minutes they soared undeviatingly, and then I saw

they had changed the plan form of their wings, so that instead of cruciform it had become a contracted anchor with broad flukes. Without apparent alteration of the axis of their bodies the birds began a stalled descent on so steeply a slanting path that my aero-plane was left well above. A thousand feet was flung to the winds as they hurtled across the last half mile to the field of plough.

Viewed from above, the rooks seemed sliding along the ground; yet they were high enough to shoot across the tall, lace-like elder flowers starring the last thick green hedge between mowing grass and plough. Indeed they had ample clearance to change from stalled flight to a normal glide as they sped towards the black congregation in the centre of the field. From my slowly circling aeroplane I watched them swing into the eye of the wind, indicated by the sun-glazed slant of grasses and leaves. Then the dark wings raked forward, tilting bodies steeper and yet steeper while the birds lost flying speed—until they abruptly landed with a hop; folded their pinions with a little shake; and instantly became absorbed in rummaging among the clods of new turned earth.

High and wide around the field I circled, engine throttled to a whisper that could not possibly disturb the birds—yet of a sudden all stampeded into flight, winging with eager strokes twice as fast as the leisured beat of normal cruising. A hundred black arrow shapes gave the illusion of using their wings like ungainly legs to crawl across the glowing, furrowed earth; yet long before the windward hedge was reached they tilted steeply in unison and in a few moments climbed enough for me to see them no longer as silhouettes, but as a great rotating cylinder of birds rising rapidly to my level. Holding my wider circuit, I watched the wild anima-tion and joyous vigour of their wing-beats, imagining hoarse screams of corvine delight drowned in the steady wind-song of my flight.

Swiftly upward swept the formation, steadily mounting their invisible circular stair. At five hundred feet the wing-beats slowed. Here and there a bird essayed to soar. Fifty feet more and every wing was held steadily as rowers resting on their oars. From a scarcely perceptible up-current, the passing thermal had grown so strong that not only had it nullified their natural rate of descent but now was lifting them at nearly two hundred feet a minute. Higher they rose and higher, until the quiet fields and trees grew dwarfed and far away. The sunlight lit the cloud of rooks with violet fire and iridescent blue. Presently they were high above me, and as I watched them circling ever higher my thoughts turned them into the satanic sable birds which years earlier I had seen soaring tropic skies.

Through the brazen heavens my Sikorsky flying-boat had crawled hopefully above a vast vista of dark forest unrolling end-lessly beneath the landward wing. Beyond the other stretched the glittering blue of the equatorial Atlantic, fringed by a yellow strip of surf-tormented beach. There was an air of unreality about it all —even though my hands held power to mount my wings to altitudes so high that they could strip the forest of inviolability and dwarf it to a panorama in which no secret distance could stay hidden. But instead, the hot and vibrant cockpit seemed the very matrix of the universe where I awaited the slow passage of time to spin the world until it brought my far and unfamiliar destination in view.

Three hours we had been flying above the edge of the ocean, bemused by burning sand, eye-aching sea, and rank green forest. For a little way we flew at fifty feet, watching the fringing palm trees flicking past. From this intimate proximity the beach stretched far and desolate and awe-inspiring—as if forgotten on creation's day, so that no man had ever trodden its lonely wind-blown sand. Beyond the feathery palms the dark forest spread omnivorously, brooding evil secrets, waiting with such menace in its stillness that presently we lifted the aeroplane higher until the unspeakable was vanquished beneath our wings. At once the beach dwindled to a frail and timid line stretching between the twin vastness of forest green and ocean blue, and the carpet of trees changed to an undulating cloak that climbed smooth hills and cascaded down the valleys. Bright flowers flamed in patches among the sun-glossed leaves. Seen from our new height, the forest lifted its greenness to the tropic sun with such disarming frankness that it became impossible to believe hot and breathless twilight reigned beneath the interlacing foliage, where million upon million insects crept and crawled and flew in a gigantic sunless empire of their own.

Foothills began to press closer to the sea, with mountains, forest clad from foot to peak, marching across the skyline in fantastic, lonely beauty, unconquered and uncaring. Elsewhere the passing years might raise dynasties or topple empires in the dust, but here in South America, century after century would find the forest still unchanged—too vast and primitive for ravaging by man, yet giving life to insect, bird, and beast.

It was then that I saw twenty great black *urubu* soaring two thousand feet above the trees, facing the landblown wind which the sun had sucked from the seas. With broad-fingered, dusky wings they leaned upon the rising air, lifting lazily, soaring the brassy heights with that same assurance of ownership which rooks and buzzards display in more temperate skies. My banishment in wild Brazil became filled with nostalgic longing for England garlanded with June. I dreamed of misty seas of springtime blue-bells glimmering in quiet woods; remembered the English flowers of summer in green fields; breathed the sharp and fragrant air of great chalk downs; heard birds singing in the dawn; listened to the muted caw of rooks in village elms. . . . I looked about me—and saw instead, twenty ominous black vultures circling un-challenged heights above an endless wilderness of green.

Such is the mind's mutability that though today I really was in England flying *Airymouse*, I was thinking down the years back to those ugly birds of prey, thought triggered by a mob of rooks lifting skyward in the self-same way. Even though both species instinctively exploited the same principles of thermodynamics their purpose was quite different. Certainly the vultures seemed to find hideous, grave pleasure in their planing; but with them, it was a vital necessity in order to attain utmost range of vision that let them spot more distant scavangers dropping miles away to gorge by shore or forest edge. If any bird was seen descending then those at the nearest stance would slant across, and in turn the next and next. Within five minutes, fifty or a hundred vultures would be tearing at the spoil which the original bird had found.

In England there are no such stringent conditions for survival, except perhaps the risk of mankind's guns and poison. The carefully tended fields are an abundant garden for man and bird and beast, so it was not surprising that every movement of the well-fed rooks expressed exuberance. Theirs was the keen enjoyment of playfully competing inch by inch for height as they abandoned themselves to the pleasure of the air pressing their wings with liquid-like solidity. Presently, with universally voiced consent, they would throw their hard-won altitude away, tearing earthwards with half-closed wings, swerving and tumbling as they played, uttering delighted shouts.

So many times my own flights ended just like that. The journey done, the test completed, the difficult moment long forgotten, I would find the familiar aerodrome once more beneath me, and feel that harbour had been reached. Like a discarded garment, the finished minutes of my flight would fade into the past as I swung exuberantly from left to right in mile-long dropping curves—or, with momentum from a dive, swept up and up once more, soaring disembodied in a sky-world brilliant with light. Impetus expended, the aeroplane would poise a moment like a crucifix held vertically in the sky, then swing over sideways and sigh towards the ground once more. Stalled turn and loop; half roll and dive; movement in compound dimension: here are the dream-smooth sequences of ballet in the air and all the pleasure of its soaring, seductive rhythm.

But now, into the stream of my thought uneasiness began to filter. With the suddenness of a spring snapping closed, it tensed to awareness of danger. Something was wrong with the engine. Reactions long conditioned and drilled to become instinctive raced to the fore. In the split second before snatching a questioning glance at oil pressure and rev. indicator, every open space within gliding distance was instantly assessed for emergency landing possibilities. Then my more calculating mind took over. Nothing faulty was indicated by the instruments—yet instinct still said there must be. I have recognized this prophetic sense of impending calamity many times, and under widely different circumstances. Fragments of evidence are subconsciously gathered, and presently their total becomes an insistance beyond the mind's logic, a warn¬ ing more and more clearly perceived that a critical change is about to happen.

So I stared intently along the black nose at the hazy greyness of the whirling propeller, and then in turn at the single cylinder projecting each side with its usual slight shake through the cowl. No sign—yet I was insistently aware of change progressively taking place: perhaps engine note, or a different pulse to the never ending vibration. I tried the magneto switches: revs. gave their normal twenty drop. Subconsciously I began to urge *Airymouse* towards the safety of greater height. Cautiously I swung her round, making for home like a wounded bird.

Scores of times while test¬flying, danger has leapt aggressively into the sunlit calm of flight. Usually I would sense the beginning of something wrong, but sometimes it was all too evident. Either way I would reduce power and speed as quickly as seemed expedient, wordlessly praying that things would not suddenly become catastrophic, and at the same time trying to diagnose the cause of trouble so that safe emergency action could be taken. Even so there were occasions when vast forces had possession so that nothing could be done except a tight¬rope act with the dice loaded against success—and if all else failed there was the chance of escape by parachute aided by the ejector seat which usually could blast the pilot free of the falling wreckage that imprisoned him.

But today there was no parachute, and this was only a slow flying little aeroplane, delicately controllable, relatively free from the vice of spinning which imperilled its ancestors of World War I, and capable of being landed in a hundred yards. So I pressed her cautiously higher, feeling it would be rash to increase power above the inadequate cruising revs. at which it was set. As we lifted foot by slow foot higher, I scanned the undulating slopes of hayfields, trying to find a meadow where the grass was short and would not pull *Airymouse* onto her nose. How small they were, and so remote from roads and help; how high their unkempt hedges! One by one I selected all that seemed possible—yet went slowly on, hoping for the best.

Revs. and oil pressure still indicated normal. I throttled a little further to ease the engine, yet could not bring myself to make a landing in this almost roadless country far from base. With remarkable intensity I willed the engine to keep its power; lifting the little aeroplane with all the force of my spirit; urging it to rise and rise, for each foot spelled a fraction of a second added to my safety. The bright mid-day sunlight that had been so blissful lined every trap and pitfall with harsh distinction.

Though my indicated height had precariously increased to six hundred feet, the land was rising swifter. I looked at the altimeter with disbelief, for evidently barely half that height separated my wheels from the ground. It gave no scope at all for choice in landing. By zig-zagging from field to field I tried to keep each reasonable chance within reach before changing for another. A minute passed. No doubt about it now: vibration was becoming marked. It would be asking for trouble if I did not immediately land. The nearest field was so dangerously steep that I let it pass. Its neighbour was a continuation of the lower part of the general slope, levelling to a narrow strip where a line of telegraph poles showed that it bordered a road. That was hopeful. Should I try?

Before I could decide the engine did it for me. Abruptly it stopped. What miracle made that happen at the only place where I had a chance of landing? With almost dispassionate interest I observed that the propeller had come off, and twenty feet ahead was sailing away and falling through the air. There was startling silence in which the wind hummed softly in the wires. Pleasure in this calm and vibrationless flight almost overwhelmed sense of danger, but mind and body flashed into reflex action. Fingers pressed the elevator control a fraction forward to dip the machine into a glide. Airspeed and the variables of height and distance were watched like a lynx. Subconscioully just sufficient pressure was applied on rudder-bar and stick to send *Airymouse* round in a steeply dropping curve that would bring the field to her.

With one clean sweep lasting half a minute, she expended her height and came sailing, as though with sense of predestination, over the tall hedge of the field I had been contemplating a few seconds earlier. For a tingling instant I perceived that the uncut hay was so high that we might be tugged to a shattering, somer-saulting stop. In the next second the wheels rasped through the tall grass by the side of the road-bordered hedge. Lightly *Airy-mouse* sank. I held my breath. Contact was imperceptible. Perhaps she ran thirty feet before the grasses winding round her axle brought her to a stop so gentle that it seemed unbelievable.

I sat listening in the unfolding stillness, absorbing the quiet, intense pleasure of being alive on a beautiful summer's day. Though there had been no greater danger than a competent helms-man might experience with a sailing dinghy in a blustering wind, this little experience heightened the beatitude. When presently I strolled round to inspect the engine in order to discover what had made the propeller fly off, I found that six bolts in the hub had sheered through and vanished, though each was supposed to be strong enough to lift an elephant. How such impossible loading could have occurred, I had no idea—but it was obvious that the engine was ruined.

Usually if one lands in even the remotest field, people presently come running up. They may be very useful. That is why in emergency I have always made it a rule to land as near a road as possible. But this time nobody came, though occasional cars went whizzing down the highway the other side of the hedge. Presently I walked the grassy verge, and within a short distance discovered the local policeman's house, only to find he was away. So his wife let me telephone home to say that I had landed in the country. Then I returned to *Airymouse*, and sat on the nearby field gate. While I waited for the car to arrive, I pondered how to dismantle the machine and get her taken away—and where could we get a new engine? Blithely a thrush began to sing from the quickset hedge beside me.

7 Laughter in the Night

It took some months to discover a replacement engine. Though it had been great fun to fly with only 38 h.p. there were drawbacks. Enticing *Airymouse* into the air after a long run across a big aerodrome was an art I enjoyed, but the insignificant power barred operation from smaller fields which I would like to use. Even when safely airborne the slow rate of shallow-angled climb could be almost neutralized by a mild down current, and on one occasion she even slowly lost height for several anxious seconds when only 100 feet up. Then again, vibration with a two-cylinder engine was so marked that sometimes I would watch the twanging wing-bracing wires with anxiety, wondering whether their thin metal connexions would fatigue and snap. On all counts more cylinders were desirable.

A suitable engine was extraordinarily difficult to find. *Airymouse* needed a halfway house between the popular Volkswagen conversion and the smallest American four-cylinder aero engines currently in production. Many letters were written. Presently I discovered that a private enthusiast had several pre-war Lycoming engines of 55 h.p., and he was good enough to let me have one.

Summer passed into autumn and faded into winter while scheming a mounting, getting the tube, building the structure, installing the engine and making new cowling.

One evening the telephone rang. It was John with a diversion. 'They're here,' he said. 'A biggish gaggle'.

'Where?'

'Heard them fly over last night. Probably making the mouth of the estuary—unless they were going farther down-channel.'

In Somerset the discovery of visiting wild geese is an event of special satisfaction, for they come only spasmodically and in smaller numbers than to the Gloucester shores of the Severn or the broad waters of Poole, and with less variety than East Anglia and the Border country. It can be a game of hide and seek to find whether any of the six main tracts of floodland and mud-flats shelter them. A breezy day may see us searching the floods from a nine-foot sailing dinghy; or in the frosty starlight, muffled with thick clothes as we paddle a canvas canoe over the drowned fields and ditches. But the most fascinating method of all is to scan likely haunts from the air, skimming individual floods in a slow-flying light aeroplane. Whatever is used, it is a rare and exhilarating achievement to find a gaggle of twenty or thirty geese.

Of all flight that can be watched from English skies, the beat of the grey goose is the most serene. With accomplished ease their wings stroke the air with a slight rise and fall that holds controlled and tremendous power. Perhaps a score times I have flown close to lone gaggles, and more occasionally have met great hosts of these migrants. As fellow voyagers for a few minutes, we have winged aloof and alone through ice-clear air above a remote and wintry world.

There have been grey-lags, with a background of snow-covered mountains ranging into the mists of the north; black brents over the sea; white-fronts above flood water and mud-flats; great estuaries with skeins of geese flying in from the sea; pink-footed geese rising in a countless army through a sky of saffron and flame as my aeroplane skimmed the seaward marshes after crossing the Wash. Triumphant moments these, each with its drama and magic quality.

Though I have often flown with teal, mallard and widgeon at heights up to a mile, geese seem to prefer a few hundred feet unless they are migrating. Only on rare occasion have I seen them above five hundred, and then they have been driven high by the roaring wind-shriek of my aeroplane. Yet, on migratory journeys they might be expected to cruise at considerable altitude, for their wings are proportioned to give efficient climb and ease the labour of flapping by utilizing soarable air. Indeed, the timbre of their calls, descending through the night air, often has a far-away quality, as though the geese were very high; but when the beat and swish of their wings can be plainly heard the birds are low enough to be within gunshot, and it becomes a sound even more thrilling than the wild music of swans.

On our wide Somerset floods wildfowl may come in thousands. Their number depends on the extent of water, and varies with the weather. A spell of fine days, following intensive rain, finds them in greatest diversity. With them on the glittering new lakes will be great flocks of swans, gulls and coot, with hosts of lapwings sharing the shallow fringes with numerous waders.

Only the seagulls and lapwings are there to herald the early shallow puddling of the water meadows near Roman Ilchester where the floods first start. Quickly the freshets and ditches pour increasing water from the higher land until an area three miles long is covered. A few more days of rain and the Yeo and Parret top their banks. Successively the wide belts of low-lying country beyond, locally called moors, succumb to the torrent rising in their extensive network of dykes and rhynes. It is as though the ribbon of time unwinds, and we see again the mediaeval meres, vast and still, which once filled all the low-lying ground of Somerset. Even the little green hills, such as the Isle of Brewers and the Isle of Abbots, become real islands just as they were a thousand years ago—and the town of Langport, standing on a bluff where the rivers join, turns once more into an estuary port. From the air each of the great flood-meres shows individual texture: some limpid clear, but tinged with silver or green; others glistening with mud, or stained with peat. The white shapes of gulls fleck each surface as though with scintillating ripples, among which swans float like great white water-lilies.

In the flooded flats below Langport the swans gather thickest. Sometimes I see them arrive in little parties, their creaking wings bearing them ponderously low above the willows. Often their flight line leads from the direction of Portland, so they are probably mute swans from the Backwater at Weymouth or the historic Swannery behind the Chesil beach. Occasionally their track has lain from the south-west where Exmouth and Teignmouth hide beyond the hills. Sometimes they sail in from the east, flying so doggedly that they may well have crossed the North Sea from far Swedish lakes where I have seen them by the hundred among broken ice as I flew over.

Swans often gather before the last grass tussocks are submerged, keeping to the deep water of the long lines of ditches which show like silver roadways through the flood. Once the meres have grown mirror-smooth with depth the swans disperse over a wider area. Then come the teal in growing parties, followed by widgeon quickly mounting to thousands.

From the air it is easy to distinguish most species of wildfowl, for not only form and colour but movement and habit help identi-fication. Teal are instantly recognized by their close clustering and diminutive size, while the manner in which the flock spring simultaneously into the air is most distinctive. They form a dusty cloud, wheeling in the distance, long before the aeroplane has reached the brief haze of ripples where they swam.

Groups of widgeon often are edged with families of mallard; yet though they all rise together in a co-mingled mass, the faster beating grey wing of the male widgeon is unmistakably different from the gay speculum bars of the mallard. So with other wildfowl—each has characteristic flight as well as distinguishing metallic-coloured feathers which show brilliantly in the sunshine when viewed from above. They may well have evolved as recognition marks.

Simultaneously with these wildfowl the coot have been arriving
—inconspicuously at first, but soon they form an army great as any
of the others. Gathering in self-contained communities always in
the shallower water, they keep well away from the gregarious
duck. From 1,000 feet their white foreheads show distinctively
from my aeroplane as it flies past at slowest speed.

While the water creeps higher yet, submerging gate tops and
fences and leaving only isolated trees, diving duck are seen for the
first time. Even though the day is so dull that their colours are
indistinguishable these birds are unmistakable, for they rarely take
wing at the approach of an aeroplane but instead float calmly
watching, confident they need only plunge to escape danger.
When the pochard and tufted duck have appeared in their first
small, isolated groups it is certain a few shovellers will arrive a
few days later. Then, at last, we begin to listen for the wild flighting of the geese.

After many years watching wildfowl, waders, gulls and swans
from the air, their habit and manner of spending the day begin to
reveal a recognizable pattern. Season after season the wildfowl
choose the same favourite pools and corners, leaving other areas
unvisited. They form a contented, quietly talkative, gay company
whose aquatic life affords a simple, carefree pattern, and for whom
the freedom of flight extends country after country as playground
and source of subsistance.

But the geese are an enigma. One day they are there and the
next have gone, leaving the thousands of wild duck crowded as
ever. The course these white-fronts and pink-feet fly is elusive as
the rainbow's end. They are rarely found in gaggles of more than
a score on the Somerset floods, yet geese find sanctuary in battalion
after battalion, both far up the Severn, on the Dumbles Salting
which Peter Scott has made into a sanctuary, and equally far seaward on the marshes of the Cardigan coast. Probably the birds of
the flood join one or other group, or there may be desultory transit
the winter through from east coast to west and back again, and in
our floods they find a halfway house. Who knows? Only by
following them repeatedly by aeroplane for a hundred miles or

more would it be possible to discover the air-routes of their choice.

It was in the early 'thirties that I first encountered birds high in the air, and began to study them in their own environment. Aero-plane and bird comply with identical aerodynamic laws: soon I began to perceive that man and bird regard flight with much the same eye, reacting with similar instinct whether scouting for a suitable landing area, manoeuvring, or finding the way. There is a singleness of design and aim in nature to which man, beast and and bird are heir. So when John rang to say that the geese were here I thought of *Airymouse* locked in the gloom of her shed, and wondered whether it would be feasible to go hunting by air again —for her open cockpit was lethally cold in winter and I regarded her more as a summer plaything.

It had been one of the wettest Decembers within memory of the moor dwellers. Despite recent dredging and widening of dykes and rhynes they soon overflowed. The floods were tremendous. True to form, thousands of wildfowl appeared as though word had spread far and wide. Cold weather followed: frost and acres of ice. Then came the report of geese. John had heard them calling as they flew with harshly whispering wings high above the southern edge of the moonlit floodlands. A week later came a day so warm that it seemed like spring. I hurried to the aerodrome and tested *Airymouse* with her new engine.

She was completely transformed. With all the zip and zest of a little fighter of the First World War she rushed wide-winged at the gentle breeze, lifting and climbing powerfully after a mere sixty-yard run instead of the long struggle her original engine used to give. This was real flying! Vibration gone; a staccato bark from the twin exhausts; slipstream flowing smooth as silk around the windscreen, icy clean and heady to breath. The red wings pressed with renewed and greater confidence on the pillowing air as *Airymouse* sailed easily above the fields, lifting the horizon in a steadily widening circle around her as she reached towards the low cloud stratus. I swung her round and about, banking from wing to wing, higher and higher. She answered like a little thoroughbred, the wind singing in her wires.

Fifteen minutes later she was skimming the glistening floods of Wet Moor, beneath the long ridgeway of Red Hill. A wisp of teal, scattered seagulls, and a lone heron took wing. No sign of geese—but I had a hunch. After a couple of circuits I lifted *Airy-mouse* in a climbing turn and raced with open throttle over the wintry country to greater floods a few miles eastward where the planted withy beds of the rural basket industry formed glowing rectangles on the silver surface. From the open centre of the floods a mingled flock of mallard and widgeon leapt into the air, drifting away like a swarm of bees. As I turned to follow their flight another line of birds flying low caught my eye. They looked like gulls in the brown and ashen dress of immaturity but their wings seemed more sharply angled at the wrist. Silhouetted in *echelon* they flew low over a meadow beyond the flood. As my aeroplane crossed their path I saw that their necks seemed longer than a gull's.

For one dramatic second the birds became so clearly focused that I could see their tails had a broad white bar, and that a ring of white feathers banded their bills.

'Geese!' I yelled to encourage *Airymouse*, and swung her into a tight turn as the great creatures drifted from sight beneath.

A full circle and we should readily spot them again, though the brown of trees and fields rather too readily matched the drab camouflage of their wings. I craned my head to look down my own steeply tilted wings as the countryside spun round the nose like a kaleidoscope. The glittering sweep of moorland flood changed to a racing vista of bare tree-tops and tightly hedged fields, a glimpse of lanes and puddles, soggy haystacks, empty meadows—then floods once more. The turn completed, I was facing the spot where the geese had been—and there, half a mile farther on and fifty feet above the water, thirty pairs of wings were patting the air with unflustered ease. I pointed the aeroplane's nose at them, diving until the wheels almost ruffled the sky reflections in the water.

Without hurry, the geese began a dignified climb. Intently I followed. A strip of sky began to show between ground and birds, for they had lifted higher than the aeroplane. Each phase of wing motion could be studied as well as the relative position of every bird in the formation. Three beats a second they made, with wingtips lifting and falling with light but powerful stroke describing arcs no more than ten degrees. From my position, a hundred yards astern, the underside of tails and bodies shone snow-white against the sky. Four seconds later, with only thirty yards between us, every bird in the formation banked simultaneously to the right and disappeared sideways under my wing. I brought the aeroplane round, picked up the geese once more, and opening the throttle, flew swiftly beneath. Peering up, I gained an impression of buff undersides barred with different degrees of black from bird to bird—but before I could be quite certain, we had passed.

Once more I rounded on them. At 60 m.p.h. our speeds nearly matched though *Airymouse* was slowly catching up. They made no attempt to hurry, holding the same light rhythm of wingbeats; yet even before the two-mile width of flood had been traversed they gained 600 feet in altitude. Only when the aeroplane sighed its way to within twenty yards did one of the geese grow nervous. With sudden lateral twist it broke formation. The others eyed the aeroplane uneasily, then canted gently away and dropped out of sight.

I made a final sally, and at 55 m.p.h., in order to hold my distance, began to weave right and left, like a yacht tacking. By now the geese had reached 800 feet but climbed no higher because of the misty cloud level resting a score feet above them. It was as though I kept station with a squadron of aircraft, for the geese having chosen their heading held it with unwavering formation. The floods which had harboured them dropped behind, but even greater stretches of water were set like casual mirrors in the dark landscape of winter ahead. Blue mist shrouded the distance where faintly the Bristol Channel showed as though it was a dull brown glaze edging the rusty-green blur of Somerset. Out there were invisible mud-flats and saltings which might well be the goal of these geese. My gaze shifted to the wisp of birds: thirty wild things disturbed from their haven, flying to another they hoped might hold greater safety.

Suddenly it seemed presumptuous to wrest the secret of a destination that their ancestors had used through many thousand years. It could be anywhere: this side of the estuary, or miles away on the other. I remembered that far Welsh inlet, grass silted and veined with muddy streams and pools, where long ago I first had the thrill of seeing grey geese from the sky. Their goal might be there or half a dozen other favoured places that I knew. Wherever it was, I decided the geese deserved to wing their way in peace, since they, and not I, were the hereditary owners of the kingdom of the air.

So I opened the engine fully, knowing we were the interlopers, and raced a last time to the geese for a farewell view of these stirring voyagers. In a matter of seconds the swiftly narrowing distance changed their thin and undulating line into an impressive formation of great creatures five feet in wing span, rhythmically swimming the air. My wingtip almost brushed them as *Airymouse* barked past. We had a swift glimpse of dark necks outstretched, and bright questioning eyes throwing a glance at each other as they watched the aeroplane. On some the loop of white feathers arching above the base of amber bills confirmed they were whitefronts. Then for the first time the formation wavered, as though no longer united in one mind; but when the leader banked away the rest followed, and I saw his beak gape wide in a great call that was drowned in the noise of my own flight.

For a few minutes I circled, looking at the subdued landscape of hills, moorside and flood. Already the gaggle of geese was diminishing in the distance to a faint line as the birds headed once more towards the dispirited shadow of scarcely recognizable, dingy sea. I stared into the mist, trying to distinguish the faint blue shape of the opposite shore. When I looked again for the geese, they had gone, leaving an empty skyway that was mine alone. I too turned homeward, and as the air-miles widened between us the geese became only a memory of birds, remaining in imagination for ever flying to the secret places of the earth.

It became too cold for any more flying that winter. Heavy frosts
followed, and the waters were ice-bound, except for small patches
here and there crowded with wildfowl. Snow fell. For many days
the world was mantled in white, so that even the frozen water
vanished except for one last pool which the wildfowl congregation kept stirred and warm. Whether the geese were sheltering
somewhere on the Severn shore, or had flown farther, no man
would ever know. They took their secret with them. The only
clue we had that the geese were on the move again was two
months later, when they were heard as they sailed through the
night.

An orange moon played hide and seek among the racing
clouds, and bathed with pale glow the Tudor walls of the court-
yard where we stood. Across the blanched lawn were soft shadows
of gable and chimney, and there was a glitter on the moat. Time
lay so still that we held our breath, almost expecting to see
phantoms glimmer and hear the rustle and murmur of the ancient
ghosts. . . . Suddenly came mocking laughter—far, faint laughter
in the night. Clouds hid the moon. From the south-west sprang a
fierce whispering, a rush of wind-drawn sound, passing overhead
with a wild trumpet cry. Geese! Laughing geese—the white-
fronted geese of my aerial hunting were returning at last to the
Arctic lands that had given them birth. The clouds drove by; the
moon came out again. The sound of the geese vanished in the
night—and I forgot that the moonlight, falling dispassionately
both on the waters of the Severn and the seas of Nova Zemlya
was a beacon to light their path, but saw only how it illuminated
an ancient house in Somerset with gentle light.

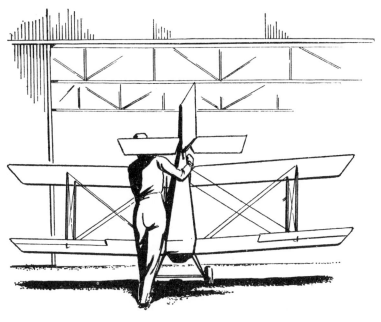

8 Glitter from Afar

Beneath a scud of low cloud *Airymouse* was lifting and rocking in the uneasy air. She was passing with marked drift above the streets and buildings of a city's outskirts, which a passing shower had left glistening in the evening light. We seemed hemmed between cloud and ground. Tired with journeying through stinging rain, I flew crouched in the cockpit, sheltering ungoggled eyes close to the oil-splashed windscreen.

In early years, before radio or other navigational aids, the wind and the rain and extent of cloud were factors decisively determining whether the day was suitable for flying. From time to time we were caught out by changing weather and required luck and cunning to bring us through. This evening I had returned to similar though easier circumstances.

From the skies one realizes how indiscriminately the rain falls— showering the crops at once place, but parching the next; wastefully deluging seas contiguous with those from which the rain had first been drawn; cascading into barren deserts or brimming tropic rivers only to evaporate long before an ocean outlet could be reached. Within the compass of a few hours' flight there could be the havoc of flood, while elsewhere the land was withering with thirst. On the endless cycle of water movement every vestige of life depends, yet despite apparent chaos nothing is entirely fortuit, ous. Implacable meteorological laws of cause and effect are as in, escapable as those balancing the suction on the wings, produced by our speed, against the downward pull of my aeroplane's weight. Similar equipoise matches the total volume of water in the world's atmosphere against the sun's heat and the surfaces of evaporation of land and sea. All round the world a long play of convection currents restlessly charges the skies, bringing vital moisture for the regeneration of life, yet equally sowing hazards of storm and fog to jeopardize man's flight as well as his earthly well-being.

Thinking of these things, I found myself idly watching the eddying little whirlpools of rainwater collecting on the wing fabric behind each lower strut root—when suddenly the tail of my eye caught sight of a great, untidy bird looming above the sea of wet roofs and chimney pots. I stared incredulously at the apparition. Ragged as a scarecrow, with several pinion and secondary feathers missing, it seemed amazing that he could fly. Yet the creature sailed buoyantly on, using powerful, easy wingbeats. His long neck was outstretched and lanky legs trailed lightly beyond his stubby tail. For a moment I watched him dwindling southward into the distance above the streets and houses. A Methuselah of herons I thought, but because we were so low I did not dare search for him above the town; so after an instinctive swing in his direction, turned back to my plotted course.

I huddled down again, playing pictures with my thoughts as I watched the wet autumn landscape slowly sliding towards me from the journey's still hidden end. Another thirty minutes and I would be gliding in to land, and the earth world would again become my familiar background. Ninety minutes more and it would be dark: I would be sitting before a glowing fire sipping sherry, the sky-world almost forgotten—this sky of scudding cloud, and misty rain curtaining the view. But that strange great bird: where would he be?

I imagined him parachuting down on stilled and hollowed wing to some quiet stream; or perhaps dropping to the tall, sway-ing branches of the cherished heronry he knew as home, where he grew from fluffy helplessness to the fierce aggressiveness of a long-beaked bird. Wind buffeted, he might at this moment be un-steadily circling, positioning himself to land. Tilting his wings steeper and steeper, he would stretch dangling feet towards the twigs. His long neck would uncoil from its arched-back position and stretch out to give better poise and view. With clumsy wing-beat and rustle of feathers he would settle, find balance, then stand inanimate a few moments except for a cautious turn of plumed head above that long grey neck as he checked whether there was danger hidden in his surroundings. But why did that picture of him seem wrong?

With a stir of recollection I realized there had been something abnormal about the poise of my ragged bird as he flew. Yes—I was sure of it. His slender neck had projected like a spear in the manner of swan or goose. No winging heron ever held it like that on a journey. From one aeroplane or another, over the years I have watched these beautiful plumed birds scores of times as they fished the dyked plains of Somerset. Within a few seconds of launching into the air every heron I ever saw invariably hunched its neck into a back-drawn curve. Like bluff-bowed Dutch yachts they would breast the air. No attitude could be more distinctive—nor if I flew alongside did they ever alter pose, despite the disturbing racket of my aeroplane. Only when landing would the neck again be ex-tended while wings and body tilted to the steep attitude for slowest touch-down.

I tried to remember the salient features of the strange, winged monster whose path so recently crossed mine. Only a ragged blur of grey remained in retrospect—that, and the sense of purpose as the great creature swam the air towards shadowed horizons which soon would be lost in dusk.

Suddenly I had it! . . . There had been March sunlight

73

painting Greek mountains with limpid clarity: purple Hymettus, Mount Aegaleous guarding Elusis Bay, Carydallus rugged and tawny, and the Thessian plain beyond, sweeping to vaster, lonelier mountains. My wing was silver against the Aegean's peerless blue, and I was peering over the edge of my cockpit at Athens, magic and remote and white, sprawling around the rocky plinth of the marble-crowned Acropolis. From nothing, from emptiness, suddenly like a flurry of snow, a host of great birds appeared. For a moment I stared incredulously, then pulled the aeroplane into a climbing turn that brought me level with their formation. Poised in the lonely sky those huge grey birds seemed creatures of mystery more wonderful and vital than all the ageless spirit of Greece over which I had been dreaming.

Unintimidated, though very much aware of the roaring mechanical monster flying so close, they continued on their way with easy wing stroke, permitting me to pass so near that I could see at each beat the slight opening and closing of their heavily emarginated wingtips. Sunlight bathed their backs, revealing the very texture of the feathers, and fell glowing on their outstretched and slightly upward-slanted necks. Three thousand feet high, they climbed steadily in a wide phalanx towards the burning skies above Mount Pindus.

They marched with clamour and with shouting like unto birds, even as when there goeth up to heaven a clamour of cranes which flee with loud cries towards the streams of the ocean. So wrote Homer. And had I not seen them massed on the mud shoals of the White Nile: grey cranes, demoiselles, storks, flamingoes, pelicans and herons?

I remembered the desolate brick-red mountains and the empty horizons of sand-desert and scorched scrubby wastes below Omdurman; the Blue Nile entering above the rapids and catar-acts; the Aswan dam; the even greater new dam; native mud huts; the blue-grey earth banks of the Nile funnelling wider; lateen sails of feluccas; Cairo gleaming in the sun; the deep blue of the Mediterranean.

I could imagine the cranes waiting like an army on the banks of the Nile delta for the dawn that would bring the right moment for the long sea crossing. Their tall forms would be dim against the stars, the clamour of their voices filling the air. As the first pale light touched the sky they would move restlessly and the babel of excitement increase as first one and then another tested the buoyancy of the air. Soon would come the sign: a moment of poised silence, and then a mighty roar of wings, wave after wave, as the waiting birds spring into the faint breeze and climb on a long slant to heights increasingly stirred by lifting air as the sun burns stronger.

When such rising air is encountered birds occasionally use pure soaring flight. More often their wingbeats are scarcely diminished. The bird slants slightly downward to counteract being lifted higher by the up current. Gravity then aids the tractive effort of the wings, the impetus of the shallow dive adding considerably to normal level speed. Using this method, and often aided by a horizontal drift of wind as well, the cranes I met above the olive plains of Greece might well have crossed five hundred miles of Mediterranean sea with ease between the spring dawn and hot noontime of my flight.

As I crouched in the cockpit of *Airymouse* the blue skies of the Mediterranean faded from memory, and I saw only the drizzling autumn overcast and the dripping rust-red trees—but I continued to puzzle over that tattered travesty of a great crane flying the English skies.

That night I wrote to the Zoological Society asking if they had recently lost such a bird. The Secretary replied: 'We have had cranes escape both from London Zoo and Whipsnade Park. I imagine the one you saw was from here. He has been out for several months, but used to come back to the Gardens occasionally.'

But would he return, I wondered; or was he flying south by east, heading across Europe towards the shores of Greece, and across the land-locked sea to where far away the White Nile gleamed in muddy *dhurra* fields abundant with food that would give tomorrow's life?

9 Operation Owl

Airymouse was homeless. The aerodrome where I had spent a lifetime flying no longer had room for her. Thousand upon thousand times I had gone winging back to that long grassy strip, confident that there was my earthly haven after the physical trial and spirit's adventuring of each flight. After so long in Eden, it was strange to have to find another place.

Many vicissitudes followed. It was remarkably difficult to find somewhere else to house the machine in a land that is all green fields and has many disused aerodromes. Even the Ministry of Aviation itself, composed one would have imagined to assist a man's right to the skies under which he was born, offered no encouragement. Nevertheless, after much correspondence, that body of disinterested gentlemen with the enlisted aid of the Air Ministry, Royal Air Force, and Ministry of Works eventually granted at a price, and provided they were indemnified for the enormous sum of £100,000 against the ravages of my miniature aeroplane, permission to use a vast rusty shed, and the weed-grown, crumbling runways of Merryfield some fifteen miles from my home. Even though critical, I was delighted. Neither the pleasure of flight, nor any other, can be measured in terms of cost. And time was slipping fast.

In post war years Merryfield had been the venue of much prototype flying for me and my colleagues. Always it had been a happy place. Even its name was significant—for 'merry' means pleasant; and the name went back beyond Domesday. Hidden from main roads on a tableland a hundred feet above the edge of the Sedgemoor levels, it was backed from south to west by the long, reposeful line of the Blackdown Hills. As a centre of operations Merryfield was ideal. Both boundary coastlines of Wessex were only twenty minutes flight distant, so on occasions I might soar those cliffs and watch their seas again. To reach the English Channel I would have to rise steadily in order to surmount the long beech crowned ridge of Windwhistle. On its other side the beautiful vale of Marshwood stretched to the southern shores in sleepy peace, undisturbed by the damaging foot of progress. If I flew in the opposite direction, dyked watermoors spread far as eye could see, their flatness softened by rounded hills and ridges rising like islands among the level green. Beyond them, distantly lit by every beam of sunlight between dawn and dusk, the bastioned wall of the Mendips lifted far across the northern horizon, shadowed with chameleon blues and mauves across its great sweep of brown and green. All the thousand square miles below that great range, from the Wiltshire Downs in the east to the Bristol Channel bounding it in the west, was the scene upon which I had gazed in flight after flight during a quarter of a century of testing untried aeroplanes.

So it was towards that long familiar northern land that I steered *Airymouse* on her first exploratory flight from Merryfield. The air was warmly smooth as I slowly flew across the wide plains of Somerset. The late afternoon sun shone softly, illuminating the whole countryside, giving richer texture to its tranquility. My small aeroplane was skimming only a score or so feet up. If I cared to set *Airymouse* a little higher I would see the bronze glint

of the Bristol Channel bounding one side of the Wessex peninsular, with the blue waters of the English Channel edging the other.
But, for the moment, it was the intimate view that enchanted me:
the breath of spring above dykes and hedges; gleaming riverlets;
new green on fields marked with tracks of cattle; and rosy willows
fringing lanes that had been raised above the water-moors when
they were first captured from the sea. The best of both worlds was
mine, for on the close reality of the living earth was superimposed
the far vista given so splendidly by wings.

With engine throttled to a murmur *Airymouse* flew at nearly
minimum speed. Despite the 50 m.p.h. showing on my air-speed
indicator, she seemed floating almost stationary upon the wind, so
that every blade of grass and hedgerow twig showed individually
before it passed from view. Maybe it was illusion, born from the
magic of riding the skies, but there seemed significance in every
patch of crushed grass, or the bare earth, or even the bubbling
eddies of the streams, because each object was seen in proper
relation to all others, like the sequence of beads on a string. They
were clues in the countryside's story of creation and fulfilment.

More than all else, as the aeroplane drifted smoothly onward, I
watched the birds: a sally of little wings from bare hedgerows,
glossy rooks rising from the wake of a plough, and the white glitter
of seagulls swimming the unsoarable air with measured wing-
beats.

At the end of winter, floodwater usually still lies upon the
plains of Somerset, forming smooth lagoons broad enough on
which to sail all day. But this year scarce a puddle showed and the
battalions of wildfowl had gone elsewhere. Today only lapwings
and starlings were disturbed in any number, though there were
small flocks of fieldfare and redwing, and it seemed there could be
none of the drama many other flights had given, when thousands
of wildfowl might rise in clouds of whirring wings, or geese lilt
across the sky bound for the brief spring of Russian shores. There
would be no adventure. I would be content with the peaceful
simplicity of this everyday English scene of waiting meadows and
quiet farmsteads and brooding time. The sky, spanning its blue

emptiness across the heights, emphasized the peace of the far hills standing sentinel above the plain, and the long perspective of fields and trees seemed a patchwork quilt draped to hide the naked earth.

When at last I turned to nearer things I found that this flight had its excitement after all—for there, less than a hundred yards ahead, a great bird was rising from a dyke. A dozen smaller birds scattered before its path.

Though the aeroplane had seemed nearly stationary, it drew up to the bird in a flash. Sunlight caught the creature. The wings gleamed a beautiful orange, patterned with purple. Frantically the bird quickened its feathery stroke, and turned so steeply sideways that all its underside showed silvered. As the aeroplane rushed past I had a split second's view of huge dark eyes regarding me form an abnormally broad head. No rare migrant this, nor perigrine or buzzard, but a creature I had never previously encountered so near in all my years of flying. Dramatically as ever the commonplace had once more become adventure.

In order to reach the fleeing bird again, I edged *Airymouse* into a turn made very cautiously lest we stall. As her wings slowly banked across the sky a snatch of conversation of a few days previously came back to me.

'There be a präpper ghostie in the churchyard, there be,' the village grandfer had confidentially wheezed.

One of the labourers sitting by the tavern fire winked slyly. 'The old man'll tell'ee a lot of nonsense,' he said.

'T'es truth, sure enough,' grandfer indignantly insisted. 'And I'll tell'ee fer why,' banging down his glass for emphasis only to whisper more dramatically: 'I *eard'n,* I tell'ee. I *eard'n.'*

He eyed the empty mug pensively. I took the hint and had it refilled with the bitter cider of his choice. Gulping it, he eyed me a little less morosely, wiped his lips with the back of his hand, and continued:

'Her hissed and snored zummat awful, her did last night. . . . I *eard'n.* . . . And I couldn't zee nawthen, though th'old moon lit church an' all bright as day. . . . T'was a präpper ghostie, sure enough.'

'He's a zilly ole vule,' the labourer said. 'Don't 'ee believe of he . . . t'were a *oyle*.'

An *oyle!* And here was I watching one as we flew: a beautiful barn owl, floating just ahead, like a great orange ghost moth drifting through the air.

It banked sharply to the left, as the aeroplane drew level, descending abruptly towards a waterbed of heavily cut withies. At the last moment it wheeled round until heading into what could have been only a almost imperceptible stir of wind. With quick breaking strokes of the wide fingered pinions it settled on a low stump almost directly beneath me.

As though riding a horse, I pressed *Airymouse* into a curve three hundred yards wide, which brought me back to the bird for further fleeting investigation. His back remained turned, but as the aero⁄plane skimmed up he twisted his head so far round that it became reversed, and the bird seemed back to front. His great eyes stared at me with thoughtful but unfrightened air. He peered up steeper and steeper, following the aeroplane as it whistled past until his head became horizontal, remaining thus he screwed it round again to the front. He did not stir a feather, until the slipstream from my propeller buffeted at his perch. His beautiful wings extended to steady him, and he floated without wingbeat onto the air.

I made another turn. Within twenty seconds I was back—but the owl was nowhere to be seen. Instead a small water vole lay dark and inanimate on the top of the stump, its life crushed to extinction by the curved and piercing talons of the hunting bird.

I ought to have realized that in the time taken for my manoeuv⁄ring the owl could not have flown more than seventy yards. Instead, I flew half a mile in the direction he had been facing, before I realized my mistake. By the time I had flown back to the tree stump, more than a minute had gone. By then it was a gamble where the owl might be, for he had all points of the compass to choose from. Therefore I cast a much bigger circle to embrace the area possible to his path. Carefully I scrutinized the ground beyond my inner wing⁄tip as the aeroplane droned tilting round with a swirl of air. The panorama of fields and dykes and hedges spun slowly with it, but no owl came in view. Once more I circled; then reluctantly gave up the hunt and swung away to see what other diversions there might be if the broadest dyke was followed.

For a mile it ran at right angles to the course I thought the owl had gone. Then it forked, and I casually chose the right hand stream. Nothing here in the form of bird or beast—only bright water eddying as it tumbled over stones and tugged at trailing weeds on its two day journey down the river-course to reach a sea that I could find in fifteen minutes. I wondered if any water-fowl might be sheltering on the estuary shores, so dismissed thought of the owl and pulled the aeroplane into a gentle climb, turning towards the glazed glitter of brown Severn water that arched the horizon like an eyebrow twenty miles away.

Before the aeroplane was twice the height of the elm trees bordering the boundary dykes I saw with amazement the now familiar moth-like beat of orange wings. I stared as though it was an apparition that had materialized from a dream. Here was another of the little miracles of flight which coincided time and place to set me on the same air path that the owl had chosen, and thus enabled me to find him once again among the broad acres of the water-moor. As though a doctor taking a patient's pulse, I counted the wingbeats of the bird. Lighter than thistledown, those soft pinions pressed the air at five beats a second. Like any other bird's they had a complex motion, marvellously coordinated by automatic reflexes controlling every feather; but where the owl differed was in the utter silence of its flight.

In detail and surface texture its wings are unique, except for the nightjar, and have evolutionary adaptations of the feathers which give that vital quality of quietness necessary to the owl's mode of life. By means of scarcely visible wing-like extensions of the barbs forming the front web of the leading pinion, the air is guided with reduced turbulence over the outer wing portion. The rest of the wing has an exaggerated downy nature which eliminates the rasping noise of the little hooks which normally hold ajacent feathers together, but which unlock and slide as the wings partially fold on lifting. In addition, each major feather possesses a silky

fringe along its trailing edge which acts like a curtain to the flow
of air, particularly when the bird hovers. Even so there might still
be noise if it was necessary to flail such wings very hard. But the
owl has big surfaces for its weight, so it is only necessary to move
them gently. However quiet and breathless the air of night, the
combination of these wing feathers enables this hunter to fly
winnowing along the shadowed hedges without a vestige of that
rush and whistle of air with which other birds give unintentional
warning of their approach. But for this, the owl would never
catch the sound-sensitive small animals on which it usually preys.

The soft-sailing creature I could see flying a stone's throw away
was also a reminder that Nature rarely closes the door on any one
line of development. That this was not solely a nocturnal bird was
evident by his being abroad full two hours before sunset; nor
could he in any way have been blinded by the light, for the vole
left on the tree stump showed how true must be his sight to have
captured it. The dykes and ditches, so far from farm and barn,
were no casual exploration, but deliberate choice of well-proved
hunting ground.

I flicked the compass ring round to align it with the track the
owl flew. My own course had edged two sides of a triangle in
following the trammelled waterway; but the owl must have taken
a direct path from the point where I first flushed him, and was
probably heading for the shelter of his home.

Disturbed by the aeroplane droning up to him, the owl turned
a little. I swung *Airymouse* round as we overshot, and made
another sally. There was a moment's glimpse of great golden-
brown wings beating the air, then the bird swerved abruptly and
shot for safety onto the bare branches of a tree. His head slowly
turned like a clockwork toy as he watched with solemn stare.
Sailing past I let the aeroplane climb a thousand feet, swung
around, and flew with quietened engine above the sheltering tree.
Feeling that the aeroplane could no longer menace him, the owl
took wing, drifting along the line of elms and making a vivid
silhouette above a green and grassy lane.

For five minutes I kept the aeroplane sweeping in circle after circle linking with the one before, yet each moving a little further forward to keep pace with the straight flight of the owl. Seven times these circles met the tangent traced by his straight and airy path. On each occasion I saw how confidently his brilliant form swept on. Even more than most birds, the coloration of the barn owl, when seen with clear light illuminating it from above, is flagrantly distinctive. The sun gives those great wings something of the gilded bloom of a flower.

With the eighth circle an ancient farmstead, an older church, and houses from forgotten centuries appeared in my line of vision instead of the owl. I looked everywhere; but the bird, after flying full three miles to my knowledge, had gone—perhaps vanished into the sheltering obscurity of a hollow tree, or hidden within the cool dimness of the church's tower.

Presently I flew back to the aerodrome and put away the machine. The evening star shone brightly as I drove slowly home, and the far hills grew deeper veiled in misty blue until they were lost in the darkening sky. The countryside closed in about me, calm and still. Earth scent filled the air, and in a little while, high over my open car roof, the tracery of bare branches showed fancifully against the risen moon, and stars blossomed on the boughs.

I garaged the car, and walked up the village street. Cottages, that had sheltered twelve generations of men and women beneath their steep eaves, stood half-shadowed on either hand. Above them the church tower loomed, tranquil in the moonlight, guarded by leering gargoyles darkly silhouetted as they leaned across the stars to drive away the evil spirits of the night. I paused, and quietness folded everything in peace. The world grew timeless; nothing stirred.

Suddenly the night was startled with a dreadful, eery shriek. For a second the stars were blotted out as an intimidating, great spectral form swept in utter silence close above my head. I drew a deep breath—and remembered the ghostie of granfer: the hisses and snores. Recollection came of the moth-like barn owl I had flown with an hour or two earlier, and I realized that he and the creature which had just sailed into the night were one with an old man's fancy.

Walking on I passed beyond the shadow of the tower, under which the ancient ghosts of grandfer's friends, his ancestors and theirs, slept a profounder sleep than any screech owl could ever wake. I looked up at the moon's white disc sailing eternal starry space—and inscrutably she gazed back at me with her Mona Lisa smile.

10 *The Game's Afoot*

That Spring it was announced a great Air Race would be held
in mid July to commemorate Blériot's epic crossing of the Channel
fifty years earlier. Splendid prizes were offered totalling £10,000,
including a £5,000 prize for the competitor who made the
journey between Marble Arch and the Arc de Triomphe in the
shortest time by any method of transport or combination of
vehicles, such as car, helicopter, and aeroplane. Although speed
of air travel had immensely increased in the last decade, the quick-
ness of travel between London and Paris had only shown marginal
improvement, so it was hoped that the competition would
demonstrate that the inter-city journey could be made in little
more than Blériot's time of about thirty-seven minutes for his cross-
Channel flight of twenty-three miles.

When ways and means were discussed with the Minister of
Transport and Civil Aviation, he enthusiastically promised: 'My
Ministry is perfectly willing to consider any idea or project . . .
and give as much help as we can.' Indeed, as *Flight* commented,

'never since the great race to Australia before World War II had there been such quickening beat in aeronautical circles, such a healthy rash of schemes and notions, or such animated buzzing at the bar. The game's afoot, and the midsummer days will be seeing such matchless deeds attempted, dared and done.'

Because I was connected with the helicopter industry many telephone enquiries came from would be entrants who thought that loan of such a machine would enable take off to be made direct from Marble Arch, with landing at or on the Arc de Triomphe, and so scoop the prize—but they presently discovered that neither the British nor the French Authorities would permit a flying machine of any kind to operate from the city centres, whether from parks, rooftops or roads, and nor would the slightest infringement of the stringent Air Navigation Regulations be permitted. Competitors therefore had to comply with road traffic and police regulations in devizing the fastest possible methods of getting through each city to the starting and terminal airfields they might select for the aircraft used during the actual cross-channel journey. The task was exceptionally difficult, for the current scheduled time offered by air lines from London passenger centre to Paris passenger centre was over three hours, and even using modern fast aircraft showed little improvement over the time taken a quarter century earlier by much slower machines, such was the ground delay due to bus ride and customs.

Westland's Battersea Heliport was placed at the disposal of competitors, so the most attractive choice became car or motor-cycle from starting point to Heliport, thence by helicopter to the nearest airfield where a fast aeroplane would be waiting with engine running to take the entrant to the nearest airfield for Paris, thence again by helicopter to Issy le Moulineaux Heliport, in the centre of Paris, and finally by motor vehicle to the finish. In these ambitious plans the R.N. and R.A.F. cooperated in offering Britain's swiftest fighters. Nevertheless, there was always the chance that fast machines might be handicapped if weather clamped, or might be grounded through mechanical trouble —so the way was open for many competitors to enter alternative schemes, which very often were of considerable ingenuity.

I began to think that for the fun of it, I might enter *Airymouse.* In the previous year her more powerful sister had been tried as a seaplane on the River Hamble using twin floats, but they proved somewhat short, cascading a bow wave which impinged on the propeller and prevented a clean take-off. When I asked if I might rebuild them for *Airymouse* there was ready assent—so it seemed the way was open to fly direct from a mooring on the Thames by Battersea Heliport to the nearest point on the Seine to the Champs Elysées.

Whatever the outcome, the idea of once more flying seaplanes was fascinating. It was long since I had handled one, but between the two great World Wars I spent many enjoyable hours with them, operating in England from Southampton Water, and on the River Plate in flights between Uruguay and the Argentine, and had brief experience with flying boats in Italy and Greece. Always that combination of skimming from water to air and back holds a quality of enchantment which none who have experienced it can ever forget. It has a poetry of sight and sound and motion that defies analysis.

My earliest experience of its fascination had been with a twin-float Avro *504*, based at A. V. Roe's minute airfield on the edge of Southampton Water near the Hamble River. These old time biplanes, such as that Avro and the Sopwith *Pup,* and presently the *Moth,* possessed such endearing qualities that they seemed the quintessence of the aeroplane maker's art. They were aerial creatures, gossamer-like, artistically built of wood, fabric, and wire instead of cold monocoque metal. They breathed life. When I first saw that Avro seaplane that sunlit morning, it was poised on a launching cradle at the top of the slipway, with fuselage tilted tail high above the long white floats, and the rakishly staggered biplane wings seemed urging it to slide down to the water and rest like a dragonfly on the smooth surface. Even as I watched there came the handling crew, clad in long waders, who kicked the chocks from the trolley wheels, and let the cradle run slowly forward to ripple through the shallows until it was submerged—

and next moment the seaplane was floating free, poised like a long legged bird. They turned her until she pointed landward, and the stem of the metal floats grated lightly on the concrete. My instructor and I stepped dry-shod onto one, and walked gingerly along its turtle-deck; climbed up the lower wingroot; and with toes in a foothole through the side of the fuselage, swung in turn into a cockpit. I took the rear position because it gave slightly better view between top and bottom wings and their steeply raked brightly varnished interplane struts, braced bar-tight with flying, landing and incidence wires. Sitting there, accustoming myself to the instruments and controls, I could feel the toe of the keel grating on the concrete and sensed how different was the buoyancy of water borne suspension compared with the very different springi-ness of a land undercarriage.

We went through the simple starting procedure. I twirled the hand operated magneto, and the engine sparked and fired, rumbling its vibration through the structure with sense of sup-pressed dynamic power. We ran it up; momentarily throttled; and were ready. The ground crew pushed at the floats until we moved backwards on to the scarcely perceptible stream, then catch-ing a wingtip they swung us round until facing open water.

'Right!' said my instructor. 'I'll demonstrate a take-off, circuit, and landing. Then you take over. O.K.?'

'O.K.!'

'We open up just enough to prevent drifting backwards. See how she is weather-cocking into the wind? That's one of the safe things about a seaplane. Always knows which way to turn . . . I'm opening up to taxy a bit further off-shore . . . Ready?'

With right hand and feet resting lightly on the controls I follow my instructor's movements. Steadily he opens the throttle, and the machine begins to surge forward, sitting back on the heel of its floats with elevator held neutral. Ten seconds of acceleration, and the trim changes—we skim the water with wings at a gentle incidence to the streaming air. The slight bumping ceases. The 504 is on her step, moving faster and faster, spray leaping from the chines, keel rasping as she lightly draws twin furrows of foam astern. More complex than driving a fast motor-boat, because simultaneous control is required in two mediums, it is easy never-theless to sense the swiftly increasing lift as the wings cushion the up and down motion, and smoothly transfer the load from the water.

'Nearly there,' comes the instructor's voice in my earphones. 'Feel it? Watch the airspeed . . . Forty . . . Fortyfive . . . A firm tug on the stick—and she's off!'

Smoothly, beautifully, the seaplane left the water, diamond-like droplets running backward along the chines and falling away. The estuary spread wider. There were ships. Calshot seaplane station showed through the hazy disc of the propeller, with the Solent spreading silvered beyond either wing, and the Isle of Wight stretching long arms westward to the Needles, and east-ward to Spithead. A few white sails were dotted here and there.

Through the smooth blue sky the Avro hummed happily, leaning her wings confidently upon the summer air. Blue seas around her; blue heights above; the green of sunlit England under either wing as we came gently round, until the fissured silver of Southampton Water notched deep into a new landscape ahead. Over the lower wing I could see lines of yachts in the Hamble River, and suddenly recognized the little slipway where we had stood ten minutes earlier. Sweeping round Warsash we curved the heaths and fields, turning into wind 800 feet above the buoyed fairway of Southampton Water. The engine died to a rumble; a high song came from the wires as we slanted towards the glittering surface.

'Important to keep dead into wind,' said the instructor. 'They don't like landing with drift. Could break the undercarriage and swing you nose in. If there is no smoke to give wind direction you can get it by watching the run of the waves.'

But there were no waves. The faint breeze did not even ruffle the surface, though I could see a limp windsock lifting enough to show we were heading correctly.

'Biggest snag is when it's dead calm,' came the voice in my ear-phones. 'Then there is risk of flattening out too high and dropping, or else you check too low and poke the floats under water. Either way its a smash.'

But for the low shore line, along which we were gliding a parallel course, I might not have known how near to the water we had dropped. Suddenly the estuary spread wide around us, and the distant view had gone. I could feel the stick being pulled back slowly in my hand, and realized that the glide was rounding off. The attitude steepened. We seemed poised.

'Back with the stick!'

There was a scrunching surge as the heel of the floats dug in, and for three seconds we skimmed like a swan alighting. Then the nose came down as trim changed from hydroplaning, and abruptly the powerful braking of the water resistance began. Almost as suddenly it stopped—and lo! we were floating placidly as a gull.

'O.K! you take her now.'

That was the pleasantest of apprenticeships. After a check circuit we taxied to the slip and my instructor got out, leaving me to it. Just as when first learning to fly, I now made landing after landing, presently extending my experience by alighting on waves made by the wake of passing ships. Finally I tried the open sea itself, learning the technique of alighting and taking off along the length of the swell, rather than imperil the machine by being catapulted into the air from the crest. Tide and wind were old acquaintances, whom I knew could be fierce enemies, but used effectively would aid success. These, and the play of light on the water, and the scend of the seas, made seaplane flying something of an adventurous gamble compared with land based operations. But if the very vastness of the open seas had an uncaring and forbidding aspect, judged by the friendly graciousness of flying over land, a magic spell was there which forever holds all air mariners.

So when it came to *Airymouse,* thirty years later, I reckoned that if I flew her full out we could go from Thames to Seine in two hours. There was no chance of winning, for as far back as 1948 the inter-city record had been set by combined use of two helicopters and a Meteor in an elapsed time of 49 minutes—or 12 minutes longer then Blériot required to cross the Channel 50 years earlier. But at least *Airymouse* could demonstrate a method very different from her competitors, and probably faster than an airline with its ground delays and surface transport. Whether I made the land portion of the journey by motor-bike or car would make little difference to the overall time—so presently I thought we might continue to be different: I would use a pair of roller-skates in order to pass the traffic jams more easily.

Before beginning the task of organizing and timing the sequence it was obviously wise to check that there would be no official snag in operating a seaplane on Seine and Thames. Both had been used for this purpose many times before. I remembered Alan Cobham coming in low over Westminster Bridge with his de Havilland 50 seaplane, and alighting in front of the Houses of Parliament where he received an official welcome at the end of his pioneer flight from Australia. It was only a little further down-river where I proposed to use the more unfrequented stretch at Battersea. In Paris friends would tackle the organization at that end, for they were just as confident of success because two seaplane companies used to have their factory on the city shores of the Seine and test their machines from the river. We began writing to the various authorities.

The Air Navigation Act forbids low flying over any crowded place, such as cities, and control zones regulate the sky routes where many airliners are sequenced to make their approach to airports such as London or Paris. However, helicopters, although single-engined aircraft, have a special concession to fly down the Thames and into the heart of London for operations from Battersea Heliport. There were no special safety requirements at that time, other than strict adherence to the river's course after a particular point of entry, even though it meant that a landplane helicopter would fall in the river should the engine fail. It therefore seemed a reasonable assumption that *Airymouse* as a seaplane, with unique ability to alight safely anywhere on the Thames, would be similarly acceptable if the helicopter's flight approach pattern was adopted.

Whom should one ask? The river here was controlled by the

Port of London Authority, though it came under the Thames Conservancy at the point of entry, so I wrote to the P.L.A. requesting permission to operate a small seaplane for the special purpose of the Blériot Commemoration Race, and defined a 100 yards of the Battersea Reach for an initial location landing and subsequent take-off. Within a few days a letter was received granting permission to use the Thames without restriction—though it was mentioned, almost as an afterthought, that if I wished to moor the machine instead of anchoring, I would have to secure planning permission from London County Council as they were owners of the river-bed. How crazy could things be? Rather than awaken sleeping dogs by involvement in such procedure, where months might pass before a decision could be given, I evolved a somewhat elaborate scheme of mooring lines between Heliport landing stage and a drogue holding the machine true. But this would necessitate permission from the Heliport owners to fit an outrigger to the structure—so complications were already beginning to appear.

Meanwhile I wrote to the Superintendent of the Southern Division of London Flying Control, stating that I was entering the Blériot Race, and that as the Port of London Authority had agreed to the flight of my ultra-light seaplane from the Thames, would Area Control define the heights and courses which I would be required to follow before turning south for Paris.

There was ominous silence. I wrote again. No reply. I telephoned—only to be told that my letter had been referred to the Ministry of Transport and Civil Aviation. At least that seemed hopeful in view of the Minister's earlier assurances when the race was first announced. I imagined his staff helpfully setting my course; but it was not until twenty-four days after my opening application that I received an answer.

I might have guessed how useless it would be. It said: 'You will no doubt realize that your proposal to land at the Heliport or on the river in Central London would not only require exemption from the low-flying regulations, but also from the Condition in the Permit to Fly prohibiting flight over populous areas. After further consideration it is regretted that the previous decision not to relax the safety regulations must be upheld. Perhaps I may also remind you that a float modification to the aircraft would invalidate the present Permit to Fly. As regards landing on the River outside the congested area, our regulations do not prohibit this provided you have a Port of London Authority permission then you can land within the provision of our low-flying regulations.'

Here were all the ominous signs of a Ministerial Department making a slow motion blockade. Time was slipping fast. Without delay I wrote contesting the logic of their reason, pointing out that single-engined helicopters already had exemption to operate at Battersea. Lest a non-aeronautical bureaucrat dealt with my letter I re-explained that my seaplane would have similar performance to existing helicopters, but was far safer for in the event of engine failure it could alight safely on any 30 yard stretch of water. Hopefully I argued that as the flight would be solely over water it could not be construed as 'over populous areas'. I also reminded the Ministry that they had permitted an Italian flying boat to use the Thames the previous year.

With almost no delay came their flattener: 'No doubt you realize that an interpretation of the legislation can only be given by a Court of Law. Subject to that, however, whilst noting your remarks I can only repeat that the Department regards the River flowing through London as part of a congested area for the purpose of the low-flying rules applicable to fixed wing aircraft'. With fine disregard for anomaly the letter affirmed that the helicopter rules specifically excluded the River as a congested area, and for good measure it added that the flying boat landed in Limehouse Reach, though it was mentioned that this was miles away.

By this time the race was less than three weeks ahead. Urgently I replied that the Ministry's letter unfortunately did not state whether I could use the Limehouse Reach, pointing out that it was enormously congested with water traffic compared with Battersea, and that there were no Customs facilities such as those at the Heliport. I stressed that it was urgent to complete plans for my seaplane entry. For what it was worth, which I felt was very little by then, I again urged that if it was safe for a single-engined landplane helicopter to fly down the River to Battersea then it must be even safer for a small seaplane. Failing all else I would agree to Limehouse.

The reply at the end of the month was entirely inadequate. It made no further reference to use of the relatively little frequented water by the Heliport, but only that they 'perhaps should have made it clear in our previous letter that permission for your aircraft to land on Limehouse Reach would not be granted.'

I was in no mood to admire the adroit delaying tactics of officials. The race was now a mere fortnight ahead. Could I press my M.P. to come to my help? Why should he be interested? What about the Opposition? Should I ring the Minister himself and remind him that he had publicly implied that his Ministry would help? When I looked at his actual words I found merely the old formula of vagueness from which escape was ever easy. The Ministry was merely 'willing to consider my project'. That word 'consider' is greatly overworked among all those we vote to rule us. It amounts to a deferred way of saying 'No'.

Meanwhile the French, with simpler logic, did not bother to hunt through every conceivable Regulation for a rule which might stop me. Had not many seaplanes and flying boats flown from the Seine within the city limits? Regardez! Had they not made hundreds of alightings? Vraiment! Then why not the little sea-plane Angleterre? Certainement, certainement!

Hastily I reconsidered plans, with wild thought of reversing the direction of the flight by taking off from Paris and alighting in one of the flooded gravel pits on the outskirts of the London Airport at Heathrow, and continuing by motor-cycle. As unfortunately entry to that area would necessitate radio I made urgent enquiries of the cost of buying a suitable set. The cheapest was £350. Installation, and wiring up my aeroplane would be another £100. I must then get it all approved by the Ministry. Despite many years of using radio when testing new aeroplanes it was decided I must sit for a Radio Operator's Examination, and the earliest would be a month ahead.

Bureaucracy had conquered in all directions! Even had there been time to get the seaplane conversion approved, obtain planning permission for mooring, secure licence endorsement to fly seaplanes, raise an overdraft for the radio, wait for installation clearance, and sit for the Operator's exam, I suppose the Ministry of Transport and Civil Aviation would have declared they had not approved the gravel pit for seaplanes, even if the London Air Traffic Controller gave radio permission to enter his area—as undoubtedly he would have done on hearing my call-sign.

Three days before the Race I sadly motored out to *Airymouse*. 'It's no good,' I said. 'We'd only have been arrested. But I doubt if Blériot ever thought of all the legal complications that would arise from that simple little flight of his fifty years ago, when he for ever shattered Britain's isolation as an island!'

She looked at me in silent sympathy. 'Let's go for a flight,' I said.

I levered open the hangar doors, and pushed her out. Swifts and swallows were circling high in the July sunshine. The engine started first swing. I clambered aboard, From a standing start in front of the hangar, I lifted her into the summer breeze in thirty yards. That was microscopic compared with the length of my selected strip of river flowing past London Heliport.

Up, up we went—the happy vista of the countryside extending wider and yet wider. In this secluded area freedom was unlimited, and from none need I seek permission to use these local English skies. I was unfettered as the birds. And there at 3,000 feet I saw a great buzzard soaring wide winged, indifferent to everything except his pleasure in the heritage that his ancestors had immemorially enjoyed.

11 *Mist Over the Moon*

In the hour before dawn there was utmost stillness. A strange radiance filled the room. Drowsily I realized that all the world outside the wide-flung casement was cloaked in misty white. No stars made music of the night, but a hidden moon filled the densely saturated air with light. All was silence and serenity. For some minutes I stood at the window, watching the invisible, lost in contemplation that drifted to nothingness.

Of a sudden the night stirred in its blindness. From far away came a plaintive call soft and clear as a distant bell. I listened, holding breath for six or seven seconds of deep silence—then heard the sound repeated: a single whistling *tlui*, distant in the west. Silence: stillness, except for the white wraith of almost imperceptibly drifting fog—and then, grown nearer, that crystal whistle piercing the night. A few seconds of waiting in silence emphasized by the faint thud of moisture dropping from the thatch, and again it came; this time very close.

I stared into the fog, half believing that I dreamed. Surely no warm-blooded scrap of feathered life could be battling across the night, calling through the sightless thickness of the fog-filled air? And did it cry in terror, jubilation, or with calm confidence, talking to others I could not hear?

High overhead, abreast the window where I stood, the bird called once again. This time not the wailing whistle, but *cour-lee-vee* it called. The triple phrasing of its notes was sweet and loud and clear.

The fog seemed to close in deeper silence on the last echoing note. I counted the seconds. At the seventh, with the precision of a sounding device, came the whistled *tlui*, but now receding in the east. Five more times I heard it, at regular intervals, growing fainter and fainter as the bird flew straight and swift towards the hidden dawn. Intently I continued listening—but the white world relapsed into unbroken silence.

I returned to my bed. Sleep was far away. My thoughts were flying with the bird. That it could journey through such dense fog was contrary to everything I believed. Full well I knew what it was like to fly an aeroplane in such conditions: the strain of concentrating on little instruments which, interpreted correctly, alone could spell safety because all sense of balance was lost in the suffocating blindness. Without these gyro controlled indicators of attitude in space, or an automatic stability system, no man could fly when view of the horizon is removed. Nor could a bird fly blind, for its senses have the same pattern as a man's. Yet what could that wailing cry portend, and why those far clear whistles spaced across the night?

If the bird was flying at some 30 m.p.h. those seven second intervals between the calls showed that its traversed a hundred yards each time. So it may have been a quarter mile to the west when first I heard it, and half as much again before it vanished in the eastern distance with cries too faint to hear. All across the sleeping land the regular reiteration of those purposeful whistles would continue to startle the night as the bird flew on and on. Perhaps, blinded by fog, it was using its ears like a radar device to pick up the echo of its call reflected from the ground. Yet that hardly seemed feasible, for I was convinced a bird has no sixth sense offering the equivalent safeguard of instruments devised by the ingenuity of man. A visual datum is essential for the ear's balancing canals to be effective. Then why had there been that wailing *cour-lee-vee* falling through the fog? I was no longer very sure of the cadence of the whistled phrases I had heard—only that they were the liquid call-notes either of a moorland or wading bird. Eventually I fell asleep.

Sun, shining through the window, wakened me. Birds sang from the hillside copse across the valley. In the far distance hung the soft blue haze of summer; but I had forgotten the moonlit fog and the lonely traveller of night. Yet within two hours I remembered it all again, and the secret was revealed. It needed merely an added factor, a different viewpoint, another slant of light—and there was no longer mystery about the bird I had puzzled over, nor of all those others which from time to time have been reported flying blind under similar conditions. Yet there was still the wonder of the great impulse which drove the birds to journey with such confidence and accuracy.

As I motored through quiet country lanes to Merryfield, the sun was coolly bright, yet slowly gaining ascendency over the cloudless morning air. I did not realize it was the day that in retrospect would mark transition from high summer to the slower pulse which in the space of another month or two would turn the leaves to red and gold—though the signs were there, for the ripened wheat glowed like burnished copper, making the yellow of nearby barley seem pale as bleached parchment by comparison. Already the mountain ash flaunted berries in the hedgerow, yet on the woodland banks gold ragwort blazed, with scabious and knapweed glowing at their feet, while on sequestered slopes fragile harebells bloomed. Tall hollyhocks stood like sleepy sentinels against cottage walls, their red rosettes and sulphur stamens bright with sun.

Swallows crouching on a barn roof uttered meditative twitters as though telling a daydream of far and fascinating places. A robin answered with short cascades of reborn song. Though almost every other bird had lost its voice, the hedges were full of their movement. The last broods were being taught to find their wings, and a sense of busy restlessness possessed a score of species, prelude to the long sequence of flights which presently would take them far across the seas, hunting in hotter lands for more abundant sustenance.

It was still early when I pushed *Airymouse* from her vast hangar, started the engine, and slowly taxied across the worn grass to face a barely perceptible south-west breeze. The noise of the engine shattered the morning peace, impounding me from the warmth of human contact. Still earth-bound, the little aeroplane lumbered forward, took heart, and with awakening determination swam lightly into the air. What I had thought imprisoning noise was instantly forgotten. I was alone, but not lonely, and this was my delightful world, new with the different enchantment which every flight brings.

Where yesterday the earth was painted with hard clear colours, today it was lightly brushed with softest blue and creamy haze. Northwards the skies were clear, but in the south distant clouds hung above a transfigured landscape where every rift and valley brimmed with white wedges of suffocating vapour. Far as eye could see there spread patches of fog, patterning the pearl-blue hills and drawing a white veil across the moonstone depths of valleys hidden at their feet.

That these exquisite shades of blue painted across a magically transformed and waiting world could be expressed in terms of moisture content, temperature gradient and pressure distribution, made them no less enthralling. Though the secret of the scene could be reduced to simple scientific fact, this did not explain why there was greater awareness of wonder and enchantment rather than of lurking peril for those who flew. Everywhere the mists were thrown casually across the landscape like a discarded bridal gown which the world had worn last night.

Last night? Steamy drifting cloud had filled the valley where I lived. The moon had suffused the vapours with filmy radiance, its translucence adding mystery to the silence of the night. I had dreamed, leaning from my window, that there was spiritual analogy in this shrouding of the world, likening it to the moments of blindness that alternate with sudden revelation illuminating the mind. . . . And then the spell had shattered as, through the still night, echoed the strange wailing call of a bird that could no longer see the familiar form of the land.

Remembering this, I looked down from my aeroplane at the half-hidden earth—then dropped steeply slanting through the ice-smooth air until we skimmed a dense cloud that filled a mile-wide valley. My wheels seemed to touch its surface and draw a trackless path along a vast and lonely glacier glittering in the sun. Yet when I descended only six feet more, *Airymouse* was ploughing through white vapours that seemed innocent enough while the light gleamed through its top, but which I knew was hiding a thousand hazards of tree and rising ground separated from me by a mere few seconds drop. With sudden disquiet at this blind engulfment I pressed on the controls, soaring a hundred feet into the unimpeded freedom of the blue above. It was just in time. Where I had been heading, a hill-side topped with a tall tower lifted above the fog, its lower slopes hidden in the opaque whiteness.

Last night I had fancied the scarcely moving mist stretched up and up, filling depths of sky until it touched the moon. Had it been some night-hour less bewitched I might have realized, from the amount of moonlight flooding through, how shallow was the cloud. This morning, from my aeroplane, it was easy to under-stand that last night's fog could have been a mere few hundred feet of moisture resting upon the ground. By dawn it had vanished from my home valley, a score miles to the east of Merryfield; but here, a little way beneath my wing, an inversion of temperature persisted, spreading like a ceiling to prevent further rising of the valley fog.

Seen from the sky last night, the world would have lain radiant white where the moon glowed down on pools of mist, with the high ground looming darkly silvered. Flying at under a thousand feet a bird would have been high enough in the clear night air to see the broad form of the earth looking almost unchanged in the moonlight from its daylight shape—with great hills rising dark on the skyline, their sequence of distinctive forms set like stepping-stones across the vales of mist. Instead of flying blind, as so incredibly it had seemed, a bird could wing its way with confidence, rising high enough above the fog to retain an ever distant view unencumbered by the hills.

Through the moon-filled sky, almost clear as day, not one bird but many might be flying separated so that each was lost from visual contact with the rest. With penetrating whistles they would call their companions—and the clear sound would be heard and wondered at by man beneath the fog.

On and on the birds would go, calling, calling. Flying by direct vision they would seek the places that satisfied their unrest, speeding across county after county, flying from the heights of Devon to Essex shores in five hours of summer's night. . . .

On the first of a flood-tide a few weeks later I sailed into a quiet North Sea creek. Among hordes of gulls were waders busy on the glistening mud-banks. Soft whistles and pipings drifted through the peaceful silence. Dunlin, running nimbly as they searched for shellfish and sea worms, rose into the air like little clouds which changed from dark to silvery white and back again. Bright coloured, long legged whimbril played rippling call-notes as they flew swiftly into the distance, and redshank newly entered from the continent lifted on pointed pinions. Sanderling flocked with them. soaring and poising on flickering wings.

In a fading breeze we anchored, and watched the placid flow of water curl and eddy past. Immensely old was the sheltered tide-way, lost in reverie of long forgotten things where once it was thronged with coastal trading ships and echoed to the creak of heavy spars as brown sails gybed to make the channel's bend.

The wind dropped and vanished. Our ancient cutter rested unmoving on the limpid smoothness of the creek. Voices grew stilled. Sea and sky were quiet with thought of rest. There was only an occasional whistle from the waders, or a subdued chuckle from the flighting gulls.

Presently I heard a soft and clear *tlui*, and then again.

'Hear that?' my companion murmured.

I seized the binoculars and searched the mudflats. A little group of golden plover came into focus—and I remembered with unexpected revelation those same liquid whistling calls which, like a far sweet bell, had trembled through the still and silent mists of night. As the dark little birds flashed into the air, revealing white underwings and a long white body stripe from head to tail, they gave loud and startled cries of *tu-tu-tlui*, and flew away with rippling song.

12 Sea Quest

I have never liked flying across open sea. The last occasion was at stratospheric height, and the big airliner, despite its 500 m.p.h., had seemed motionless at the centre of a hollow sphere of melting blue, composed of cloudless atmosphere imperceptibly blending into an identical blue of unrecognizable ocean. All was a timeless negation in which a void of blue sky balanced on the blue emptiness below. Sunlight piercing the cabin windows of the flight deck fell warm upon our faces. Eyes were half closed against its blinding brightness. Enfolded in secret thoughts we sat there, absorbed and silent, indifferent that the atmosphere on which the great wings seemed to rest so solidly was in fact so thin that life was unsupportable, unless air was forced into the cabin at great pressure in order to acquire breathable consistency. During the hours we sat there, sky and sea remained blue nothingness—yet in that time, believing the unbelievable, we traversed an extent of water greater than Columbus voyaged in primitive faith for as many weeks.

On earlier occasions I had flown at lesser heights across seas that similarly diffused their horizons into the softness of the sky. Before aeroplanes had blind-flying equipment a foreshortened, false horizon of this nature gave no sense of the aircraft's attitude in space. Under these conditions I have seen a great battleship apparently sailing the sky high above eye level—only to realize with a jolt that my machine was slanting from sky to sea because I had failed to observe the unwinding altimeter. In such moments one realizes overwhelmingly that the sea is an enemy, pitilessly ready to exterminate; only with later aircraft did one learn to ex-clude impressions of feeling and outward viewing, and instead implicity trust the artificially correct horizon of a gyro instrument.

To take the almost instrumentless *Airymouse* on a direct course across the mist-veiled Cornish Sea, from Rame Head to Dodman, was a gamble which a pilot of my years should have ignored in the interest of safety. As the empty miles sped by I listened with keyed up intensity to the engine as though it might stop at any minute—for land was beyond reach of my glide. I was back in the primitive time of Blériot praying his little three-cylinder engine would keep going long enough to carry him across the Channel; or Hinkler struggling to Australia as he hopped from one im-provised landing place to another, using a light plane powered with the converted half of a war-time engine; or Hawker, who had to ditch in the open Atlantic when the single engine of his Sopwith stopped, and he was rescued by a miracle. But the difference was that they blazed trails which later became prime airways of the world—whereas I was merely being rash, impelled to fly some way off-shore because the seas had always been a chal-lenge, however much they enthralled with peace and beauty or terrible and menacing power. In another thirty minutes I would show *Airymouse* where this unbreakable bondage had begun.

Already we had been flying an hour before reaching the sea. The flood of high summer was high and hazy over hill and wood and field, creating reflection of the long succession of men and women who had shaped the land and given England its indivi-duality. Century after century, passing like drifting clouds, had left a glimmering impression of ancient ways and long gone passions, hinting of struggle, regret, of peace and hope. From the shape of the present there distils a veil of meaning giving comprehension of the past, so that as I gazed down at misty little villages and old townships I seemed to understand the secret of their repose. Yet there were harsher lessons if one wished to understand. It was no good shutting eyes and imagining everything was orderly and safe. The peaceful fields were a delusion. Man was recklessly poisoning with chemicals a world that was not his own. This was the era of specialists, who saw no further than their own devices. Even the heavens were being impaired with fission fall-out and growing deposits of untold tons of jet and rocket fuel which presently might impose disastrous climatic effects because they barred the sun. There was no escape from the misbegotten horrors of this age into the seclusion of the desert, nor by sailing into the loneliness of an ocean, or climbing to solitude on a mountain; one could not drug oneself with music, nor seek safety within a citadel of brass. Security went with the advent of the atom bomb— itself a symbol that man has become a merciless machine, letting loose forces beyond control with utter disregard for the future of every kind of life. Within closed walls, behind locked doors, there is a rustle of secrecy: a tearing of treaties, thumbing of contracts, scrape of legal tomes, counting of bank notes, complacent breathing, hum of computers calculating the corruption of the world. Yet man the hunter, man so greedy, so cruelly plotting, apparently so indifferent to his fellows, can be a creature of idealistic aspiration whose badge is courage and whose need is peace in which to flower.

Two thousand feet beneath my wings I had seen Plymouth Sound glimmering through mist. Between its shores and the russet hills, a hundred thousand houses spread a shadowy blotch. That was the hand of man in all its smugness—but it was also his home, his hope, his life. And there at his door was the sea: his challenge to adventure, and the field of achievement which established the Britain in which we live.

Upon the green space of the Hoe, among the milling throng of ant-like people and stream of cars, I could just perceive the statue of lawless Drake. By his very character he must have impelled his group of rough, tough men to set out on that great adventure into the unknown of sailing for the first time round the world. No charts, inadequate compass, neither chronometer nor sextant; certainly no radio with its unhurried voice directing a course of safety: only faith in an idea, and confidence in himself. If Drake could sail armed solely with his valour, then surely I could make this little crossing of the sea from the dark pyramid of Rame Head to St. Anthony's light thirty miles on?

So into the summer-misted blue of sea and sky I headed *Airymouse*. Glittering like silver fish scales in the south, the water reached from emptiness towards me, deepening in colour as it passed rippling towards the rocky shore of Cornwall. With slight apprehension I watched the cliffs recede, more and more lost in haze. Wider, emptier spread the blue nothingness—remoter the grey-blue land. As the miles slid by, I began to visualize each hidden haven on that coast. Set in narrow clefts above their massive granite breakwaters, rows of grey, white, and colour-washed houses have watched for more than four hundred years the long play of the sea on the mauve and green-bronze rocks, while their harbours growled defiance at the gigantic, gale lashed waves.

I stared at the empty sea, and felt its menace reach towards me with hungry fingers. Intently I listened through the harsh roar of the slipstream to the beat of the engine, taking the pulse of the tense tremor it made in the structure. All was well. No need for disquiet. But because of my familiarity with the sea I could not disregard the threat of those deceptive depths. For eternity the waves had rocked with uncaring rhythm over the drowned bones of uncountable age and youth. From the sky it was impossible to forget the hunger of those seas—yet sailing these same waters through the surge of summer, one's heart is filled with peace, and the unfolding wake whispers promises of happy immortality.

By now land was ten miles abeam, with the long inlet of Fowey Harbour hidden in the haze. Even as I tried to locate it, there materialized through the veiling haze the dark shape of a steamer, made beetle-like by our height and distance as it headed out to sea with vigorous determination. For the moment it spelled safety if my engine stopped, though calm reasoning told me that contingency was most unlikely. Nevertheless a score of failures leaves me distrustful of all engines. Nor have I any illusion about ditching on the sea.

From the skies it is forcibly brought home that the globe is a world of water. A scattered quarter of the earth's surface, comprising the total of all continents and islands, thrusts fractionally above a flood of water which already has engulfed the land more than once in the long history of evolution, Unaware of the peril of his tenancy, man sees the crumbling rock, clay and chalk as secure and indestructable. From stratospheric skies, let alone the orbit of a spaceman, it is clear that land is only the low, irregular summit of uprisings of the sea bed. No longer do the great promontories, from Cornwall to Hatteras, seem granite bastions of overwhelming grandeur, impregnable to storm and tempest, but appear frail walls, crumbling and torn, fit to endure only a short time relative to the gigantic scale measuring the vast past ages.

Looking at the mist-shrouded water from far lower height at which *Airymouse* was flying, I almost shuddered at thought of the billions of years the sea had lain there, sullenly heaving, eternally waiting, while uncountable organisms of life lived and died and dropped and dropped like falling rain into the primeval oozes of the ocean bed. With compulsive caution I again checked the oil pressure, glanced at the petrol indicator, and stared into the distance at a faint shadow of land on the horizon, wishing I was there and that this foolish run, far from the illusory safety of little fields, was over. And yet the fascination of the sea held me in its grip, as though I was a gambler whose fate depended on the spinning wheel.

Down there, a curiously thick consistency of the water confimed we must be about mid-way across St Austell Bay. The sea had lost its inward glow and was stained with the clay that is endlessly being loaded at the long, whitened stone quay of Par— the one port in that long and rugged coast with little charm. By contrast Mevagissey, a few miles on, typifies the very spirit of ancient Cornwall. Mist hid the little bay where that clustering township snuggles beneath a great green hill, flanked by dark and savage cliffs which prelude fierce and pitiless rock that presently takes battle against the whole force of the Atlantic. From the sea on a day of storm the fanged granite of those wild headlands seems the very antithesis of hope—yet from the high sky they are nothing.

Presently I began to distinguish from my winged isolation that the misty loom ahead was the Dodman—that last great promontory before Lands End. All unconsciously I had been pressing slightly on the right rudder pedal because it brought me to quicker reassurance of the shore. The engine took firmer note. I leaned past the windscreen into the wind. Sunlight was driving away the haze and spangling the far water with sparkling waves of clearer, deeper blue. Beyond Nare Head the quiet fields of St AnthonyinRoseland began to appear, and behind them the sheen of Falmouth steadily widened.

From *Airymouse* I looked down at the old familiar anchorage where my enthralment had begun. It was unchanged. The harbour water stretched far and smooth and glistening, pressing gently between the bluffs of St Mawes and Mylor on opposite shores, flowing inland and streaming silver between deep woods crowding to the water's edge. I watched the shadow of my aeroplane turn round and slide down the Fal, then drift across the harbour towards the sea. In ten minutes more we would land, and the shadow of my flight would join the shadows of the past, obliterated like the cleft ploughed by the keels of ships in the moving waters of the world.

13 Dusk Flight

Flying the starlit darkness always had compelling attraction for me, though occasions were all too few. Given the assurance of radio and multi-engines the unity of dusky earth and luminous sky holds such calm beauty that it drives loneliness away. Gold, white, green and blue—the lights of villages and cities and long highways are scattered like jewels in strings and loops and clusters across the blue-black darkness far below. Above them a palace roof of stars burns with more individual brilliance in the thinner atmosphere of great heights than when viewed from the earth. Vast powers seem to reach down from the heavens, enfolding with such deep peace that new realms of inward vision are revealed. The world becomes forgotten—until an engine falters; the radio fades; ice glitters on a wing; or cloud, looming like a mountain of blackness, blots out the stars. Then instantly we become mortal: tense and beset with peril; body and mind seeking the way of escape that will bring back the world.

Night flight with a machine powered by only a single engine

has more complex aspect. From the first movement of accelerating into the ever receding blackness, there is uneasy awareness that the engine may fail at any moment and a blind crash-landing become inevitable. My lack of faith in engines has spoiled many a brief excursion into the moonlit night—yet the attraction of those skies has still been undeniable. The higher one reaches towards the stars the more they lull sense of insecurity. Yet however much the starlit, moon drenched night captivates the heart, presently cold logic urges that a single engine is an unwise gamble. Back to the earth one speeds with a strange mixture of relief mingling with compunction at fleeing from adventure. Nevertheless, in retrospect there is a warming knowledge that even attempting so cautious a flight helped the spirit grow in stature.

So with recollection of these things I plotted to re-experience them in smaller way with *Airymouse*, and lashed red and green torches to the respective front struts of port and starboard wings, adding a plain white pointing rearward from the fairing behind my cockpit. Then, as early evening stole across the sky, I switched them on and climbed aboard, while Andy waited in my car so that presently he could set the headlamps to illuminate a landing path across the grass.

As my small aeroplane lightly lifted from the first few yards of runway, and left it still stretching a mile onward, the little fields and farmsteads of Somerset tilted into view, and all the slowly dimming land breathed sleepy life. I headed north across the low escarpment of Red Hill, and found floods, smooth as mirrors, on every water-moor. Always the rains seem bent on re-establishing the old pattern of the land, where centuries ago the hills encompassed a broad but marshy inlet of the sea. Three days of heavy downpour and the surface water of the hills had found the bowl of the moor, brimming the freshets and brooks and filling the huge system of dyked ditches until they flood their banks long before reaching the broad main rhynes and rivers which eventually find the sea.

The mists of evening were closing on the land, painting the winter fields with chalky blue, above which the far hills rose with

starker outline than in the equalizing light of day. A soft grey haze
of cloud began to drape the thin transparent blueness of the sky—
but where the hidden sun's last rays lit the west, a crystal luminosity
bewitched the air and glazed the clouds with palest gold. Presently
we turned slightly, making a different angle with the floods and
saw them change their silver for the glowing softness of the sky's
reflection.

With muffled engine, *Airymouse* sighed her wings at the steep
incidence of slow flight across the first quiet flood, and dropping
lower, skimmed the next. Four hundred yards ahead the water's
molten smoothness stirred into a passing instant's rippled pattern
as a thousand wildfowl leaped into the air with powerful leg
thrust and violent beat of wing. Like a swarm of bees they drifted
in compact mass from our line of flight—but before we had
crossed the breadth of the flood they slanted to the water and were
once more swimming in close packed company. Even as *Airymouse* flew across the drowned fields and headed towards the
River Isles where it ran clear of the floods I saw, hiding beneath
the rim of its nearest bank, two men with guns peering through the
grasses at the clustered birds on the nearest of the submerged fields.

Suddenly one of the wildfowlers turned, and settling gun on
shoulder swung it towards a swan majestically approaching from
the remote end of the flood, flying parallel with the river bank
and a hundred feet high. Perhaps the man did not intend to
shoot, and sighted his gun from boredom, but without waiting to
discover the intention we dived across the path of the great white
bird—for the swan is a noble aeronaut, and it was bitter shame
that he might die in his glory. With scarcely perceptible change in
the synchronized speed of wingbeat the swan thrust vigorously
with his left pinions and swung hard away from the aeroplane,
putting himself far beyond shot range as he swept over the floods.

Up sprang the wildfowl at our new intrusion, but we disregarded their massed flight and I again throttled in order to follow
the swan and ensure he got out of harm's way, though I overlooked
the fact that the bird knew his intended destination and would fly
on regardless of danger.

Away went the swan, great wings bending at the tips as they repetitively slanted powerfully down, then lifted for the next stroke, cutting diagonally through air of almost liquid consistency at the speed at which we flew. My scarlet *Airymouse*, her wing lights glowing, was two hundred yards astern, still losing speed yet slowly catching up, though the engine was only windmilling, giving the propeller a darker blur than the hazily spinning disc of its usual speed. Steadily the airspeed fell; slower and slower we crept towards our quarry—until suddenly I saw we were holding distance, and it became necessary to have more thrust from the engine to keep up with the bird. A hundred yards astern I sat in the sky, gently juggling the throttle and subconciously giving the gentle control movements necessary to hold the aeroplane in precise station. Speed was exactly 45 m.p.h.

Knowing from the wind-rushing noise astern that he was being chased, the swan swerved ten degrees right, and then to left. His wings were flailing faster than a gull's and with increasingly powerful movement. Speed crept up to over 50 m.p.h. I could see the bird's head turn slightly so that his brown eyes could watch me. Concentrating on exact formation with the dominant white shape of the swan. I scarcely regarded the dimming, flood-filled land even in broad outline. I only knew that we had turned a right angle, slowly climbing as we headed towards the Isle of Muchelney where it rose hog-backed from waters pressing close on either flank.

Suddenly the bird canted in a tighter curve than any aeroplane could follow. For a moment I saw the swan's vigorous profile, and the great forward throw of its wings on each downward beat—and then we had overshot. With quickened interest I saw that it had a black beak: a Bewicks'—not a mute!

The swans which in their hundreds visit the winter floods of Somerset are chiefly semi-domestic mutes, which fly in from a wide area, and many seem to come from the Swannery at Abbots-bury. Each secluded flood area gets its colony of twenty to fifty, visible in their startling water-lily whiteness from as much as 20,000 feet above. Whooper and Bewicks' are rarer birds, recognizable from mute swans by greater readiness to get airborne when disturbed by an aeroplane. If the two wilder species are seen together the Bewicks' is the smaller, and when viewed from an aeroplane passing close by, it often can be confirmed by the black appearance of its beak compared with the yellow of a whooper's, where only the tip is black.

I let my tilted turn swing further towards the majestic creature, and opened the engine. With fifty yards separating our parallel courses, and *Airymouse* no more than a stone's throw behind, the swan with unexpected suddenness turned defiantly in a tight half circle towards the aeroplane. Wildfowl, geese and all smaller birds invariably seek escape by swinging at right angles onto a course which takes then quickest from pursuit—but occasionally a swan, like the eagle, vulture, and many hawks, may eventually turn at bay, overcome with irritation at the persistence of an aeroplane which can match with another manoeuvre every one of theirs. It is no mere bluff, for tropic hawks have been known to attack.

The Bewicks' swan, flying six hundred feet above the floods of King Alfred's lands, gave only an angry glance and lashed the silken air more furiously with intimidating wings. Bird and aero-plane crossed less than twenty feet apart, yet were separated by half a mile before I could turn a semi-circle in order to follow once more. The swan became ghostly white in the misted distance, high above the tired green fields; turning to a snowflake above the black furrows; was almost lost against the silver background of the floods. Each time I re-located the bird it was flying swiftly and purposefully into the west. The engine deepened its enfolding snarl. Slowly the speed crept up. When seventy miles an hour showed we began to catch the swan, and presently could decelerate to our old formation of hundred yards astern.

Two long minutes we stayed together. The swan was like a racing swimmer, thrusting with tremendous force. Our airspeed held steady at the still considerable speed of sixty m.p.h. Then with the same unexpectedness as before, the swan turned imperi-ously towards the aeroplane, banking a majestic circle. Instantly

I pulled higher—and from vertically above had a moment's unique glimpse of the great bird painted with incisive detail as it pressed powerfully upon the air.

Opening the engine fully I climbed higher still, turning the aeroplane enough to watch where the swan might go when no longer in peril of pursuit. Already it was far ahead—a white flower blowing in the wind, drifting downwards in the middle air between the higher trajectory of my wings and the darkening misty ground. Lower and lower with every wingbeat dropped the bird, steering steadily away from waters dotted with other swans to where the floods were empty and the scene austere. Skeleton trees and tangled black hedges threw reflection instead of the clear pattern of more burnished water—but the wild swan perceived that here was lonelier seclusion than anywhere else in those floods. Downwards he drove, half circled on wings fiercely inclined to give sudden resistance, steadied and slowed, and with stilled wings went skimming the last hundred yards, then fanned wide his tail and tilted at steeper and steeper incidence until a long bow wave suddenly rippled. An instant more and the swan was floating calmly in the shadowy reflection of a hedge.

Earliest night was stealing across the waiting countryside, obliterating with duskier blue the faint outlines of the distant fields. The clouds were smoky grey where, ten minutes earlier, they possessed a last sheen of pearl. From the great flood waters every vestige of gold had ebbed, so that they became vast stained puddles brimming in a strange land of muddy earth and lifeless yellow grass. Impalpable curtains drew across the diminishing horizons as mist thickened in the evening air.

With a farewell glance at the harboured swan I turned the little aeroplane for home. Throttle fully open, we raced the last of the dusk, speeding back towards the dark floods where the wild-fowlers had been encountered—only to fly onwards imprisoned in the opaque atmosphere, the earth but dimly seen. I sat there waiting, listening hopefully to the magnified racket of engine and shriek of air, yet knowing that presently the minutes would bring into view the unmistakable street lights of the town that would tell me my airfield was near. Into that void of unreality I flew with no glance at the compass, assured with undeliberating confidence that we headed accurately to our goal, reading every scarce-seen road and hedge and stream as though it was a signpost.

More pin-prick lights; more golden windows. There slid into steadily enlarging view the massed lights of the town I sought—yellow, blue and white, glittering and spelling home. A mile away Andy's two headlamps cut a swathe of illumination across the aerodrome. With suddenly released exuberance I pulled *Airy-mouse* into a light-hearted climb. Only then did I realize that the clouds had parted, and the sky was already bright with stars.

Night, I have come back to you! I can relax because the airfield is near. Even should this little engine stop I am safe. The age old peace of the stars pours down as I fly the edge of the invisible abyss above a deeper darkness profusely scattered with the warmly coloured, pin-point lights of man. The rigid features of his civilization are mantled; hidden. Conspiracies, intolerances, inhumanities, have vanished. There is only the glowing husk of the world, the infinity of stars, and what seems the supernatural sanction of a different purpose. I ride the silence humbled by the impress of immortality in the vastness of the constellations. . . . And yet they are friendly stars: Dubhe white and bright, close to man's guide Polaris scintillating low above the northern horizon; Arcturus more brilliant still; Cassiopeia among the myriad dust-stars of the Milky Way: red Aldebran burning near the ten small stars clustering the Pleiades. Perhaps some other time I might find opportunity of one more flight, and once again find Sirius, most beautiful of stars; or make a journey high above the moonlit fields to reach the golden moon path rippling across a silvered sea. Perhaps. . . .

In the pool of darkness below my wings car lights flashed on and off as though Andy wondered whether I was lost. It jerked me to reality. I throttled back and gauged the point where *Airymouse* must turn to make the landing path precisely.

The little aeroplane came sighing down, its wing-tip lights far deeper coloured against the opalescent sky than any stars. It landed with a gentle, hollow rumble on the turf, and taxied to the concrete apron with Andy driving close behind to light the way.

'That was grand,' I said as I climbed out.

'Would you like a mug of tea?' was his reply.

I nodded. Already the sky world had become unreal. The mystery and the wonder had never been. The earth was firm beneath our feet. Above our heads a cloud began to drift across the stars.

14 *Flamant Rose*

From the field in which I landed, my yacht was visible resting quietly on ebbing water that slid mirror-smooth between mud-banks glittering in the setting sun. When *Airymouse* had been picketed for the night I strolled towards the Sailing Club, only to encounter Paddy hurrying to meet me.

'Me bhoy—if it isn't yourself that I was wishing for!' he called.

'And why, my son?'

'You wouldn't be wanting to hear about the bird I saw not an hour ago?' he asked with tantalizing air. 'A great one it was—and coloured like fire!'

'A swan in the sunset', I suggested.

'How could that be?' he demanded, 'for I saw it all red against a clear blue sky.'

'And how did it fly?'

'I've never seen the like before', said he. 'Uncertain, slow, as though it searched; and then the cräture swept round, still glowing like a rose—and presently was gone.'

I looked up at the evening sky. Soon it would be twilight. Paddy followed my thoughts. 'What's stopping you, me bhoy? There's light enough. Just fly that little plane of yours once round, and you'll see my bird on some mudbank as aisy as can be.'

'Paddy,' I admonished. 'You're sure it was a bird, and not some winged creation of that Irish mind of yours?'

'The Saints forgive ye,' he made reply, and took my arm to hurry me.

Five minutes later *Airymouse* was racing across the small rough field by the water's edge, and with a last little jump became air-borne. Reaching for the evening skies she skimmed smoothly a few feet above the rivulets and runnels of the madflats and then began to climb. Gulls on lazy wings drifted away to right and left. Scuttering waders flailed into the air. A gaunt heron tumbled into flight, departing with ruffled dignity to more secret shallows. With every second the expanse of mud and glittering water spread wider.

Scarce had 500 ft. been gained than the hidden sun lifted a gold rim from the north-west horizon, below which it had settled ten minutes earlier. The sky around it seemed relit with tender light—but the world beneath my smoothly sailing wings lay etched with stillness. Across the eastern sky I saw a dusky veil was spreading.

Tall masted yachts at anchor showed small and toy-like for a moment, their crews gazing up. They vanished, and we were crossing Swears deep, heading aslant the brown stream of the main channel to the other side. Close umder my wing the shore streamed past—a patterned repetition of green weed fringed with stranded flotsam on mudbanks curving up from the edge of shallows marked at intervals with poles. Inland, the quiet fields were set with elm trees from which rooks tumbled on dark wings. More and more gulls, oyster catchers, curlews, sandpipers, rippled into the air ahead, only to wheel round and land after we passed. Their small star-like footprints on the mud might be seen for an instant set with microscopic precision in all that broad pattern of estuary spreading its four-mile course to where banks of yellow shingle and a faint tumble of white marked the harbour entrance. The silken line beyond was open sea. But of the rose-tinted bird there was never a sign.

The land ended, and there was only rippled sand, around whose lip the sea swept towards far inland reaches where many yachts lay still as resting butterflies. I could see that there the water became a broad river curving through a park-like countryside, fair with meadows and full-leafed trees.

'Not a sign,' I shouted to *Airymouse*. 'We'll try the other side.'

The tilting wing seemed to brush the water with its tip as I swept a wide curve away from our former course. The harbour entrance, and the darkening sea outside, slid sideways beyond the whirling propeller giving place to steep piled shingle on the western shore. Within its sheltering arm more yachts lay ready for the night, their anchor lights like stars. But *Airymouse* turned further still, drawing an arc across more distant sand dunes and the sea beyond. Scattered houses came in view; drew closer; became a little town set beside sands lapped by calm waters spreading like a broad lagoon from the dark loom of the far Isle of Wight. Round we came, and now the first lights of Portsmouth twinkled ahead, with Langstone harbour a silver twin of Chichester, and the dusk-filled fields of Hayling a barrier between.

When I looked steeply down, the wet acres of ebb-drained mud were patterned with filigree patches of green weed upon the glistening brown. Everywhere white wings, grey, speckled brown, pied or black, scattered into flight—but never a wing of fiery pink beat into the air.

Muted to low power, the engine drew no echo from the quiet world. Like a great ghost-moth *Airymouse* drifted upon the un-moving air of dusk, following the deep indentations of the shore, while I scanned each waterway and inlet with dwindling hope. By now pin-points of light were appearing far away beneath the purple shadowed Sussex heights. When I looked high at the darkening skies the first faint stars were there.

'Have to give up'. I told *Airymouse*, and opening the engine we climbed a thousand feet above the darkening world. The dulled land seemed breasting the waters of the sea—a crouched and might form, hinting strength and wisdom, guarding a heritage beyond comprehension of time. Even the jewelled strings of lights added emphasis to the immortality of the earth. Yet when sudden uneasiness made me glide down lest my unlit landing field vanish in the dark, the land of indistinctly shadowed fields and shrouded trees already had become uncaring, brooding dark secrets of its own. But I was almost home—the quest forgotten.

I set the little aeroplane quietly gliding so that it reached the dusk-blurred landing field and skimmed the hedge at precise speed and height for a gentle touch-down just beyond. The swish of air on wings and propeller faded; the lightly jolting wheels rumbled to a stop. I switched off the engine. The evening light had almost gone—and suddenly the still air thrilled to the bubbling cry of seabirds, wading distantly on the mud. While we picketed the aeroplane, twilight gave place to starry night.

As we walked back to the Sailing Club, talking with subdued voices that matched the hour, Paddy pointed far down the dark estury to where the star Antares glowed, faintly ruby red to the south. 'Faith—if it isn't my bird,' he exclaimed, 'flying far over the seas to his native land!'

'The spirit of your rose-red bird,' I echoed—and looking at the red star flying through infinity could half believe that Paddy's fantasy was true. Had not I, on one of my earliest journeys to France, followed an aerial path that took me to her southern shores where secret places guarded a township of great birds that I had thought was a carpet of pink flowers?

In that flight of long ago, when the sky was a new strange love with whom it was enthralling to be alone, I had taken off while the world was still asleep, and climbed to just below a great cloud strata that hid the early summer sun. Dull-hued and cold, Southampton Water slid diagonally beneath me and was replaced by the Isle of Wight, dark and rain-sodden beyond the propeller's shimmering disc. Presently there was only sea, unfriendly and grey; then threatening broken cloud began to form beneath my wings so that I flew as though through a tunnel of vapour. Above and below, the grey and suffocating cloud imprisoned me with an unreality that echoed madly to the engine's reverberant din. We had neither radio nor traffic control those days, and only know/ledge that the meteorologists promised clearer skies the other side of the Channel prevented me turning back. Nor was it easy to believe that the unwavering point of my compass promised the path of escape. Flight had the confusion of a dream, until suddenly a shaft of sunlight pierced the haze and showed a great shadow on the water—and I realized this was Guernsey, and that my course was true.

Once more the clouds closed in, but I flew with stronger faith —on and on, keeping a wary eye on the grey overcast that, five hundred feet above my aeroplane, endlessly sealed the sky. When I looked beneath my wings patches of dull glazed sea occasionally showed between rifts of draggled cloud. Time stood still. No longer was it a stream taking me from one minute to another, from one place to the next. My aeroplane was suspended eternally in space. England was a memory; France a name upon a map . . . With an effort I checked the compass course, and for the hun/dredth time looked at oil pressure and revs.

Yet soon the clouds began to melt, vanishing from the sea, turning translucent above me where previously they had been opaque. Shadowed though the water was, it now showed great patches of blue not far ahead; and ten minutes later the sun was shining from an azure sky in which great cumulus were sailing. Low upon the horizon, clear and finely drawn, lay the longed for shore of France. I slanted down, joyful to exchange height for speed. The coast rose high; the sea vanished—and lo! the earth, the sweet smelling poignant earth, lay beneath my racing wing. The familiar illusion of fulfilment returned, and against it no remembrance of danger could prevail.

Purple moorlands and the rugged hills of Brittany aflame with gorse greeted me. Low I flew across the heights, then skimmed the countryside southwards, flying with intimate nearness to the ground. When I lifted higher it was to see far on the western horizon the Cape of Ushant like a mirage where the land angled sharply to begin the vast Bay of Biscay. Half an hour more and I was following its indented shore 1,000 ft. above. A wild wind sang in from the Atlantic, and cascading up the cliffs lifted me still higher above the gulls soaring their face. Great waves surged from the fullness of the ocean and broke into a thousand frag-ments on the dark rocks at their feet.

For another hour I flew dreaming along the coast of France, building from my thoughts an empire of romance. Presently a growing doubt intruded. Fuel was running low, and the military aerodrome I needed had not yet come in view. I began to scan both countryside and map with anxious eye.

Two hours later—the machine refuelled and I well fed, mortal in a world of men—the spell once more embraced me. Far under-neath my V-strutted wings the face of France was open as a book. I flew above a countryside where slumbrous townships and magic castles dreamed among fair fields and tumbling hills. Mine was the great migratory highway of the birds, following the Garonne southward, and then the silver thread of the Canal du Midi. Cypress began to replace poplars and plane trees, and soon I was aware of the Pyrenees looming in the hazy distance like a great blue wall.

I altered course away from the forest foot hills, and steered more directly for Marseilles. The land was burnt and brown beneath the brilliant sun. Presently a different land replaced it—an olive green wilderness, desolate and primitive, of mud and waterways and great salt lakes. I stared with fascination at these legendary swamps of the Carmargue heralding the vast mud-islanded delta of the Rhone. Suddenly I saw that one of the islands was brilliant with flowers. Long and narrow, it was set in a lonely lake, and shone as though covered with giant chrysanthemums of fire-flecked glowing pink. In keeping with the swampy mirage mists it seemed to materialize from nowhere, and then was gone. Indeed I would have forgotten all about that smudge of colour among the mud and reeds had I not met a Frenchman in Marseilles that night whose passion was flowers.

'Tell me,' I said as we sipped red wine on the balcony of the

Basso restaurant, looking across a sea of dark roofs to the silhouette of the surrounding mountains and Notre Dame de la Garde outlined against the starry sky, 'Tell me. What is the bright pink flower that grows in the swamps of the Carmague?'

'You mistake yourself', he replied. 'In that place there are no such flowers.'

'But I saw a whole island of them only this afternoon.'

'An island, monsieur?'

I nodded.

'It it possible that you mean the Flamants Roses?' he asked.

'And what are they?'

His eyes twinkled. 'It is well that you ask,' he said. 'The special peculiarity is the structure of the bill, which is large and abruptly bent down at the middle . . .'

'You mean they were birds?' I interrupted.

'It is so, monsieur. They somewhat resemble geese and are coloured pink with vermilion wing coverts.'

'Flamingoes!' I cried. 'Flamingoes in Europe?'

'It might be that they were, monsieur. It might well be . . . Yet many mirages are in the Carmague, which make possible what is not, and hide what is there.'

He raised his glowing glass to mine.

'Flamants Roses,' said he.

'The island of rose-coloured birds,' I replied.

15 *Forenoon and Afternoon*

The clock on the dressing table insisted I had overslept. Cloud hung low above the valley, and dull grey mist thickly hid the larch woods flanking the steep hill opposite. I scrutinized the overcast for a ray of hope, for I had planned a little flight to Weston on the shores of the Bristol Channel, where gliding friends were holding a sailplane meeting. Instrument flying rules were im-practicable because *Airymouse* still had no radio, nor were her instruments adequate. But I knew the route like the back of my hand, and as there was no local problem of flight traffic areas an attempt seemed worth while.

When I arrived at Merryfield the great black hangars on the other side were dimly discernible shadows. No sunlight penetrated the clouds or thinned the vapour. Yet the gloom seemed safe enough, for the slow speed at which *Airymouse* flies gives ample time to spot obstructions, and her small size and nimble control enable her to throw an easy circuit of 50 yards radius if it is necessary to turn back and seek another way when there is danger.

So I got her ready. Rather than set a course that we might not be able to keep, I turned the compass true north for orientation and cautiously took off, but once airborne felt more hemmed in than I expected. Left and right and dead ahead were walls of blue-white mist. Dragging wisps of cloud, a short way up, warned that ceiling had been reached. Trees lost their third dimension, and became flat silhouettes, set in staggered rows like stamped lead toys, dwindling in clarity. Only immediately under the aeroplane were trees and fields and roads clearly visible, as one by one they drifted past like eddies seen from a low bridge, each giving a moment of speculative interest.

The first five minutes would determine whether the journey was feasible or not—for we were heading across the slowly rising tableland that sweeps to the long ridge of Redhill, whose northern face abruptly drops 200 feet to the flats of West Sedgemoor. Once skimming the moors, things should be safe enough if I ruddered somewhat to port, for only a little westward of our track ran the rail line from Taunton to Weston, making a unmistakable guide-line we must not cross.

A little tensely in the enveloping, datumless mist I held *Airymouse* at 400 feet by altimeter. It was easy to imagine spectral obstruction of tall trees or latticed pylons as the rising ground came gradually nearer the wheels; but uneasiness was counteracted from moment to moment as I recognized here a farm, there a haystack, and at last the grey main road heralding the steep declivity to the dyked meadows of the water-moors.

It seemed thicker here. Hopefully I steered through misty nothingness to where the Mump, a small conical hill crowned by a tower commemorating King Alfred, should soon distinctively show near Athelney. I ruddered a few degrees further west to ensure that I did not run into it, but even as the magnetic needle obediently shifted past the grid mark I spotted the River Tone, which I knew was near the hill. Barely half a minute later came the blurred but familiar landmark of the Frome/Taunton railway line running parrallel with the road to Glastonbury. Of Athelney there was no sign. It was lost in the mist, and my blind flight must be midway in the ten mile channel of low country between the dangerously tall bluff of Aller Hill somewhere away to the east and the remote edge of the Quantocks lost in the west. This meant that five minutes ahead we would have to surmount the western bluff of the invisible Poldens lifting in a long ridge 300 feet high athwart our path. Perhaps it would be better to veer slightly east again in order to locate the unmistakable straight ditch of the great Kings Sedgemoor Rhyne, then follow its course towards the westernmost edge of the Poldens.

In the small cockpit of my aeroplane it was difficult to use the map, but now and again I had to glance at it to keep the disposition of hidden obstructions in mind. It was with relief that soon I saw the misty runways of Weston Zoyland airfield set like a great dark cross ahead of *Airymouse's* nose—and there, away to the right as it vanished into the mist, spread the long, straight channel of glazed water which was to be my guide.

Every sluice and ditch, almost every patch of weeds in this four mile stretch was familiar because, for many years, this long canal had been my measured run when testing the speed of prototype aeroplanes. Old type biplane, low-winger monoplane and parasol, early autogiro, and tail-less fighter, even the first aeroplane to surmount Everest, had skimmed this waterway where quiet cattle stared up from lonely fields, and herons lifted on slow, grey wings. The rhyne at this end made a distinctively sharp northward angle, and then edged the sodded fields where Faversham and Churchill once pitted their skilled troops against the undisciplined valour of Monmouth's men, and routed his initial triumphant progress to the throne. Today it all lay drab and drear; insignificant despite the desperate past.

Slow as a moth in the dusk, we followed the line of green water, striking diagonally north by west. Again I glanced at the map, and saw that at any moment a railway bridge would cross the rhyne, and at that intersection a tall line of northward marching power pylons struck across them. To dodge this peril I ruddered hard right, towards the mist-hidden hills, and found the railroad cutting through a notch in the Poldens, leading to the safety of the other side. A moment later, the ghostly pylons groped their steel arms menacingly through the mist at slightly lower level. Instinctively I veered away before forcing myself to follow their live cables in certain knowledge that they set a path far easier to follow than any that radio compass and blind flying instruments could have offered. Like hypnotic shadows in an empty street, each latticed tower and swathe of cables loomed and vanished through the mist. Listening to the steady staccato of the engine, my thoughts played hide and seek while my outward eye watched the undeviating pylons march one by one implacably toward me, only to pass and leave my aeroplane unmoving upon the mist.

In this enveloping, foggy nothingness, I am imprisoned within myself, yet dramatically conscious of the eternity of time. Like an uncertain whisper I hear the past; far and faint as dawn I see the future. But here am I, lost from the world in whitely hemming isolation, bereft of my fellows, divorced from their life, yet living an identicallity of time. I am not discouraged by this moment; not frightened by it, but in a lacuna where thought drifts through echoing white emptiness; speculating, analysing; building a logical picture from signs and portents; living the reality of compass and pylon path, revs. and oil pressure and pulse of engine. Mind and senses send swift impulses compelling hands and feet to maintain an almost imperceptible juggling which keeps my little world of wings flying without catastrophe—like seeking an attitude of life affording balance between have and have not.

I glance at the clock. Time soon must bring *Airymouse* to the formidable barrier of the Mendips: maybe in another three minutes. If I have faith, these power cables will guide me through a valley that breaches the towering range into twin hill-sides. Anxiously I peer ahead. Almost at once a dramatic blue wall of hill with hidden top thrusts through the mist. The trigger of danger snaps the machine into another abrupt turn before I realize that the range must still be half a mile distant. When I look at the map for reassurance it seems that the track I intended to follow will trap us in a gully of the hills where the Lox Yeo River rises. Deserting the cables, I cautiously edge westward along the hazy bulk of the Mendips, trying to believe that presently I shall reach the unobstructed safety of the sea. The confluent waterways of Yeo and Axe, curving at the foot of steep Bleadon ridge, became my guide.

All that nearby coast had been my friend during two decades of testing aeroplanes, particularly in later years—for as higher speeds and great wing-loadings evolved, the risk mounted when engine failure necessitated a forced-landing. Every prototype I flew made at least one perilous return to earth because each had a new type engine that was largely untried in the air, although it might have had several hundred hours of bench running. So Berrow Flats, towards which *Airymouse* was now heading to round the Mendips, had long been an area where I made the more hazardous tests because its miles of open sand offered superb safety in a belly landing. Today, as I reached the low shore I smiled at recollecting the discovery that one of my fellow pilots held the same view.

Clamped in a terminal velocity dive on that occasion, with seat set low and head bowed to avoid being hit if the canopy came off, I suddenly heard Roy's voice on the radio giving a routine call to base that he was diving. His machine might be anywhere within the fifty miles range of his broadcast, so any attempt to spot him would be useless, yet I felt compelled to lift my seat and look outside—and was appalled to find him hurtling past in similar blind headlong dive from the opposite direction, and vanish far below.

I called 'Hi!' on the radio.

'Struth! You startled me—where are you?' he asked.

'We just missed diving into each other—you blind clot!'

'Struth!' came his voice with considerable feeling as I began to pull my machine level from its maximum dive speed:'We're, getting dangerous!'

Our task was to discover whether the big contra-rotating twin coaxial propellers of our identical fighters could stand repeated recoveries at black-out accelerations. Already three of my com- panions had lost their lives testing this type of machine, and we needed to prove that the involved technical problems had at last been safely sorted out. Between us, Roy and I made a thousand dives before the technicians called it a day—and by that time we could not have carried on much longer, for the physical strain on heart and brain tissue was intense. It was many weeks before we felt normal again.

Months after that diving incident I was flying in this area on speed trials with the same aeroplane. Blue and empty and endless were the skies at 30,000 feet. I seemed to be the isolated centre, of the space world around me—though occasional voices in my microphones revealed the impersonal chatter of other men flying unseen, ten, twenty, or even a hundred miles distant; yet there was always the possibility that they were close as Roy had been. But solitude enfolded me, and the snarling thunder of the engine beat against the streamlined Perspex canopy of my cockpit as though a titanic waterfall was crashing down a canyon. I began another speed-run. Because aeroplane and I seemed one, I became instantly aware of a slight alteration in the throb of vibration. A moment later, almost as though I expected it, came a subtle change of tempo—nothing much at first, but enough to make me quickly close the throttle and pull off speed. Like a tiger crouching, the creature instinct within me felt the cold breath of the unknown— that fog which in a blink of an eye could curtain the sunlight of morning forever, and extinguish my life.

Far below the solid looking, massive wedge of my fighter's port wing I could see a small rectangle of yellow, fringed by a swathe of chocolate sea, which almost unbelievably signified the five mile length of Berrow Flats. If there was trouble, that was where I would have to bring this heavy monster down, sliding on its belly at 100 m.p.h. across the sand—for it would be disastrous to extend the wheels as they would sink deep, and turn the machine over. Danger froze inhibitions to an icy calm. I began the sequence of safety checks. Almost immediately the oil pressure began to drop.

I radiod base . . . No answer. After waiting an irretrievable minute I radiod again . . . No answer . . . Forget it . . . You are in big trouble. What shall you do? That great stretch of sand you always had in mind for moments like this is easily within reach. Yes—but you will damage this unique machine: break its £10,000 propeller: wreck its wings. You may clamber ashore, but the tide will presently submerge the aeroplane. Nothing could be recovered from that soft sand and mud.

We dropped from 12,000 feet to 5,000 feet in less than two minutes. What ought I to do? Should I take the easy haven of those sands, or could I just make the runway of Weston Airport, whose open space I could clearly discern four miles ahead? That was the way to save the machine. With reasonable luck I could pull off a normal landing with wheels down—and then, when things had been put right, presently fly the machine home. Or was it just that little too far away? . . . Quick! Which are you going to do? Which? . . .

But already I was sweeping the fighter in a broad, steady curve towards the leeward side of the Airport, eking the glide with a little power—watching the ominously falling oil pressure, every sense alert to the grating pulse of engine and propeller whose freedom to revolve depended entirely on that oil.

Set just as things were, though faced with necessity of maintaining a little power to flatten the descending path, I could see that a fair curve would bring me finally into wind in time for a last brief straight that would place the machine nicely on the runway. I partly put down the flap to give more lift, saving the overwhelming air resistance of the undercarriage for last minute lowering as a brake when I was safely centred for touch-down.

Like a great bird, the heavy torpedo-fighter came canting round, dropping fast, until at 600 feet we were on the last lap. Even as I straightened her, scarcely two thousand yards from the beginning of the runway, I felt a subtle change in the hardness of the vibration: it became thicker, uneven, shuddering more heavily. Power was dramatically fading. I glanced at the oil pressure. None! Simultaneously the engine grated to a stop—the eight paddle blades of the double propeller stayed fixed at their flattest angle broadside to the wind, giving such enormous drag that it meant plunging the nose down at 30 degrees to retain safety speed. Hopeless, hopeless! Fields and hedges flung upwards. Impossible to reach the airfield. This is where we crash. Each field is tiny—fringed with hedges and ditches. Impossible to touch down safely, let alone stop within the length of four.

Yet my eye instinctively had picked out the only safe line. One moment we were 200 feet up: the next 20 feet. Straight at the narrow bridle-path across a bridge I set the nose. Parapets on each side scraped under the scything wings. A small green field opened. Clods flew up as the lower blades of the stationary propeller ripped the turf. Back with the control column: a sense of smooth contact—and the machine was catapulting on its belly at tre-mendous speed towards a gateway in the hedge 100 yards away. With a crash the nose burst through the exact centre of the gate. The oak posts snapped and pierced the metal wings as we sliced through thorn hedges each side and jolted over a deep ditch. Across the next field swept my unstoppable wreck: through the boundary hedge and across a still wider ditch: pitched abruptly steeper on its nose—and came to rest. Dramatic silence: stillness: sunshine: life flowing onwards and outwards again. I unbuckled the tight harness straps and jumped hurriedly onto wings that were flat on the ground. Only then did I see flames licking from the nose. Why had the automatic extinguishers not operated? I tore off my parachute, rushed up the footsteps, groped for the fire extinguisher buttons, and pressed—then dropped down and took cover behind a bank waiting for the explosion. But the flames died out. Relaxed and grateful in the peace and sunshine I waited twenty minutes before anyone reached me.

When later I told the retrieving crew that in the end she caught fire, the foreman laconically said: 'Well you might just as well 'ave let the bastard burn. T'would have saved a mint o' trouble.'

And now here was I in *Airymouse* flying through the murk seeking that same airfield after a lapse of fifteen years. I stared right and left, trying to pierce mist which seemed a little thinner. A restricted circle of rippled sands spread beneath, and landward I could just discern tall houses. A moment later I passed Weston

Pier, and began banking seaward to clear the tall promontory of Worlebury Hill rising steeply above the town. Far on the other side of the water the Severn began to glitter as though the sun at last was burning up the fog. Wider and wider spread the horizon, washed with ever paler mists, but as I swung back towards the land the white curtain hung down impenetrably as a wall. Cautiously I headed towards the town, picked up the railway line, and with relief found the broad expanse of aerodrome. As I edged round the hangars and came gliding down to land, the rough fields of my war-time experience were hidden underwing in the pearly mist.

'Temperature inversion.' they said when I walked across to the row of sailplanes resting on tilted wings.

'It's beginning to clear over the estuary,' I told them.

'That's what Met. said,' they agreed, then added hopefully: 'There is a snake's chance of some launches this afternoon, but it isn't great. What about a drink?'

The afternoon drifted away in hazy sunlight. A few launches were made, though with little success. 'We'll have to scrub,' they said.

So I started *Airymouse* for home, and as we climbed the ice-smooth air I found that visibility had enormously increased, so that far into the distance green fields stretched misty-blue beneath the paler blue of sky on one side, and on the other the velvet browness of the Bristol Channel. Ahead towered the steep, tree-covered, northern slope of Bleadon Hill preluding the Mendip massif lifting high and dark across the south-east. Through the shallow valley between the forest tops of Bent Hill and Banwell we sailed, and found our old friend, the great line of marching pylons, athwart our course in the Lox Yeo River valley. On both sides and ahead was the main bulk of the Mendips. As *Airymouse* crossed high above the railroad I saw that it entered a tunnel almost directly below to emerge in a declivity breaching the south face of the Mendips. We followed its direction, flying level with the downland tops on either side, though the altimeter showed 700 feet.

The structure of these Mendip Hills is the oldest in Wessex, for the red sandstone base of the loftiest parts lifted three hundred million years ago. Fifty million years later the flood water of the world left them covered with carboniferous limestone, which millions of years of seeping water riddled into caves and swallet' holes which presently became the home of Palaeolithic men. It was the roof of one of the bigger caves that eventually weathered away to become the deep and winding Chedder Gorge, but as I banked round the great curve of Chute Shelve Hill by Axbridge, and entered the Somerset plain, this great rift was hidden by successive indentations of the steeply rising southwest face of the towering range stretching away and away into the distance, until it blended with the Wessex chalk heights.

Yet it was not the heights which held me today but the broad vale below the Mendips. Far into blue distance spread the water' moors, flat and unchecked except for the Polden Hills midway in the south, almost reaching my hidden landing place at Merry' field. The misty evening, made golden by the slowly sinking sun, added magic to that great green plain. East and west and south, far as eye could see, lay neat, flat pasture land, framed and criss' crossed with long straight rhynes and ditches of silver water. Long ago I used to fly across those water'moors in early morning, and a rolling sea of mist would cover them a few feet deep, so that the conical knoles and narrow slivers of hills became islands lifting in solitude from white lagoons, just as they used to among the waters that once covered this land. Silt and peat and pasture now lie over the old sea'bed, and cattle browse where men used to fish. Lake villages, encampments and even boats have been dug from the soil. On occasion I have landed by helicopter at an excavation site, and seen pottery, quorns and fish hooks still half embedded in the earth; and once I watched from the air the thick peat of today being dug away to expose the faggot foundations of the great causeway, called the Abbots Way, where priests used to walk the long path westward from Glastonbury through the bogs and marshes.

It is always the green hill of Glastonbury, lifting boldly from the plain, that draws the eye from whatever aspect or however far it is seen. It is the symbol of a country of legend, of mystery, of priests and kings—and the great skies seem to stretch above it with calm beneficence. As I looked down from *Airymouse*, tree and field and water ditch shone with cool, collected brilliance—as though harbouring secret immortality, sprung from the living pulse of centuries of prayer and longing and fulfilment.

Swiftly the Tor, crowned by the ruined tower of St Michael, came nearer, dominating sky and land with air of serenity and continuance. Its legends may be disbelieved but they are a signpost, for in mediaeval days this hill with its nearby Abbey was the most important in the length and breadth of England. From all the known world came pilgrims, priests, the rich and poor, the humble and the proud to pray before the golden shrine where Joseph of Arimathaea preached that God is love. Man may forget; but the great hill retains its overwhelming character and hallowed air, so that even the winds seem to pass on tiptoe lest they disturb that dream of long ago.

I turned *Airymouse* away from ruined Abbey and vanished Palace; away from the memory of King Arthur and his Guinevere awaiting in sleep the time when England once more needs them; away from the echo of unending footsteps, the age-long whisper of prayer, the pennants bravely flying and the flash of armour as knights go riding. Smoothly sailing the aerial deeps we flew high across the sunny land of Avelon 'fair with orchard lawns and bowery hollows crowned with summer sea', and headed across the Polden Hills to find Aller Hill rising nobly above the water meadows of the twin lands of Kings Sedgemore. On its top I could see rough marks hinting the story of rich Britons who adopted the Roman mode of life in the fourth century and built a fine farm-villa there. One bright winter's day in earlier flying years I happened to look down from the cold open cockpit of the sedate *Wapiti* biplane I was testing, and saw on the snow-covered smoothness of the hill a large rectangle distinctively marked in shadowy blue upon the whiteness. I puzzled a while, and then forgot it—but years later I visited the site, and found archaeologists excavating magnificent mosaic floors depicting Dido and Aeneas hunting, and Trojan Triremes rowing into Carthage harbour. In the great villa which they unearthed, a long line of patrician owners had lived until the Scandinavian savages infiltrated Britain and destroyed a cultural way of life. Deserted Roman villas, like many a later English mansion, tumbled into ruin or were pulled down stone by stone, vanishing in half a century to leave only a scar on the enfolding turf. So here.

As I looked from *Airymouse* at the scarcely discernible rough-ness on the ground, Rome slipped astern—uncaring that I had acknowledged it. The high distinctive hill dropped steeply to let the multitude of water meadows regain brief possession for ten miles, before ending at the long cliff-line of Redhill walling the southern end of the Somerset plain. I had almost completed the circuit. There, beyond the Isle of Abbots and the Isle of Brewers in their sea of quiet green, were the sheds of Merryfield, just distin-guishable as small rectangles against the background skyline of the Blackdown Hills. Like a moth in the evening air, *Airymouse* quietly flew to her home. With a sense of happy familiarity she circuited, and came sighing through the quiet sky to land on the sixty yard strip of rough grass by her hangar door. The Merryfield of my departure in the mists of the past had become the welcoming haven of evening. I climbed out, leaving helmet and goggles in the cockpit. All was still. No bird sang, nor was there anything to break the silence except the faint sound of an occasional bell from sheep grazing at the far end of the airfield. On tiptoe I put *Airymouse* away. It signified that yet another quiet adventure was hidden by time beyond today, like a half remembered poem in a quiet book of verse.

16 Swallow Wings

Under the fierce sun the earth grew listless. The sky was brazen. Shimmering with heat, the air expanded in great bubbles that rose into the heights until their rate of cooling equalled the temperature lapse rate of the surrounding atmosphere. There they floated for a while, blending with the general drift of air, before diffusing and slowly descending to complete the convection cycle and presently start anew as an uprising current.

The faint trembling of the air gave no further hint that inexorable forces were at work. Yet the whole economy of the countryside was affected. Although no ground breeze stirred the summer heat, the drifting thermals carried skywards untold myriads of minute winged insects, ultimately spreading them further than the most ambitious striving of their normal flight. So light were these specks of life, that they floated higher and higher to the topmost limit of the up-currents, until at last diptera, thrips and aphis came gently parachuting down—ten, twenty or even a hundred miles from the blighted crops or eaten leaves and flowers from which they first took wing. I know, because I found them—high in the upper air.

They were not visible from my aeroplane as they flew: their little bodies would have been more insignificant than dust against the vastness of the blue. Instead, during a hundred miles of morning flight I only knew they were in endless groups at many heights because my aeroplane became spattered with tiny bodies. Their gauzy wings, each the forlorn symbol of a miracle of creation, fluttered in scores upon the Perspex windscreen, streaking it with the scarlet, green, or gold essence of their life force.

When at length *Airymouse* landed at her destination, I found she was thickly coated everywhere. Before washing down the wing leading edges and white struts I counted the blotches and mangled filaments which had for so short a while been unpresuming life. An inch wide strip the length of the port wing contained more than a thousand bodies. So on my four leading edges four or five thousand were heaped, and thousands more were crushed upon the struts, wires, propeller, windscreen and engine cowling. Yet it was not only the huge number I had snatched from the high skies but the diversity that amazed me. An entomologist could have found infinite treasures of deduction in the intermingled fragments of *maxillae, elytra* and *chitin;* but alas, I had insufficient knowledge to identify the genera. Resting on the turf in the shade of my wings, the task of cleaning done, I pondered over the ten thousand little bodies whose vital spark of existence had been swept away. Tall grasses, sprung from the alchemy of orderly decay, moved lightly above my pillowed head, and all the air was filled with quiet murmur of winged things infinitely small. When I turned on my back and stared beyond the aeroplane's wing into the high void above I saw swallows hawking, swinging from turn to turn with lightly pattering wing.

Two hours later *Airymouse* was droning homeward. Steadily we climbed until the aeroplane was floating on a full mile's depth of air, and familiar illusion tricked my passivity into belief that the machine stood still while the wide panorama slowly unrolled below. For a long time I flew with contented interest at the unfolding of seven English counties. I saw their curves and secret beauty. The sun assuaged them. Drowsily they dreamed.

Winging in happy solitude I forgot men and the creatures of the earth; nor did I remember the transient specks of winged life who were fellow voyagers in the vast air ocean through which I flew. The little cockpit in which I sat was warm and bright with sun, insulating me with a cocoon of millimetre ply from the smoothly rushing air outside. Even the dull diapason of slipstream roar and engine din became a soothing murmur, like the opiate of waves breaking upon the shore.

Presently I seemed to waken from the soporific that lulled my consciousness, though I had been well aware of making routine checks of engine instruments and compass, and even glancing at the map. I looked around. The modulation of the land was no less harmonious, but now I saw it as a carefully tended garden. Trim meadows and ordered arable made a theme of glowing green in which hedge and tree, full-leafed woods and slender spinny, new-sprung corn and ripening grass, spread in sunny perspective until they dissolved into the green-blue blur of far horizons. It was a world of waiting stillness, proudly indifferent of man's control though superficially subservient. A neglect of man's handiwork, and the wilderness would snatch back its own.

Looking down on the vastness of the living green, I saw the careful cultivation, the neatness of the wide-flung net of hedges, the wandering lanes, half-hidden roads, dwarfed cottages and houses, the little fields where scattered groups of cattle grazed with quiet engrossment—but of man himself there was no sight. Even when I flew above a town, whose length of serried streets would take half a day to walk, it was transfigured to a mere few minutes blemish, insignificant among the endless verdure.

As though demonstrating its primitive origins, the land abruptly changed, halting the rich meadowlands and abandoning the trees at the foot of a chalk escarpment. On the bare heights the rolling downs began sweeping to new horizons, forgetful of the old. Far as eye could see spread the kingdom of the vanished Celts, where men and women of high artistic culture lived all unwitting that history would one day end their world; but now fine grasses and sweet herb-flowers sprang from the soil that hid their ancient bones.

Airymouse rocked a little as she flew high above the beginning of those smoothly curving downs, for their sun-warmed slopes reflected a different heat from the alluvial lands we were leaving. I felt her lifting. Almost immediately a scattering of sharp winged birds flashed into view, soaring level with my windscreen. An instant only, and then they had gone; yet within a minute I flew through a crowd of others, passing so close that it was easy to see the jewelled blue of their iridescent wings.

In the pellucid atmosphere of the upper air, light falls on the top surface of a bird's wing with a brilliance rarely found at ground level in northern lands. Seen from the skies even rooks and crows, which normally look darkly black, become lustered like the blue of night, or may glitter ghostly silver in a momentary reflection of slanting light. Bird when viewing bird sees the other's characteristic colours glowing like a rainbow, as if their markings were painted and patterned specifically to give immediate recogni-tion of sex and breed.

Though the only pigments in feathers are black-brown to yellow, the rapier wings of the swallows soaring level with my aeroplane, a mile above the sun-bright downs, were bluer than the deepest seas because light played on the ridged polygonal cones of the horny sheaths to give new opalescent depths and shades with every tilt and twist. When the birds turned away, their wings and bodies for a flashing instant changed to silver-white flakes spark-ling against the sky's blue.

Another cloud of swallows appeared, and we sailed a narrow passage through them so close that I could see the spasmodic opening and shutting of their long forked tails as they sought to trim the changing lift forces made by each minute adjustment of their flickering wings. The tilting, circling, erratic flight that every bird displayed was ardent as the sun itself. Their purpose was intent, yet full of joy. The aeroplane did not disturb them in the slightest. As still another swallow flashed above my wing I saw the needle-beak agape, the glittering eye—and then the bird was gone. . . .

But in that second of movement I had understood why the birds had climbed so high. I realized that my windscreen had again become lightly spattered with similar coloured juices to those of the outward flight. Risen to yet greater altitude, the insects of the morning were still fulfilling a destiny that was inescapable. Carried, whatever their will, high in the torrent of uprising air, their memory of the earth-world and its scented flowers was drugged and lost in the slow anaesthesia of exhaustion as they swirled through the dizzy, oxygen starved vastness of the heights.

With all life Nature is utterly profligate. What matters the individual if the species lives? Yet despite her prodigality she is frugal. If she deals death to some it means life to others. So million upon million insects were playthings of the sun's caprice that day—and in ones and twos and dozens, until there were a thousand here and there, they fell easy prey to hawking swallows using the same up-current to aid their climb into the upper sky.

Every now and again I could see a bird poise for the open beaked snatch. Their wings would throw forward, tilting the body steeply upward, the tail fanned wide and acutely depressed to hold the attitude. Whether success or failure followed the attack, wings and tail instantly closed, and the swallow again picked up the light beat of level flight. They rode with easy eagerness the high summer thermals, their movements winged with quick precision, carefree with a happiness that differed from the supreme ecstasy of nuptial flights.

My aeroplane went thrusting on, leaving them to their hunting. Presently they would be surfeited and swim the buoyant air on planing wings, uttering from time to time sweet quick chattering. Not until hunger was satisfied, or thermals failed, would they go slanting and curving down a twenty mile air slope, back to the barns and farmsteads of their terrestial life.

I looked down the glide paths they might take. Almost the full extent of downland could be seen with even the most indiscrimi-nate glance. Far west and south it stretched to the commencement of another faintly visible chequerboard of meadowland. No buildings could be distinguished, but the swallows would fly as confidently as I do when, unguided by map or compass, course is set for a destination hidden beyond the horizon's edge. It is not inexplicable intuition, but a facet of the mind's ability to adapt itself to every circumstance with such lightning speed that it seems pre-experienced. With the sun used subconsciously as reference point, landmarks become stepping-stones, making it easy enough to fly the skyway in the requisite direction whether or not one has previously travelled the route. True I have studied maps and by such visual communication know the shape of the land; but birds have power of aural contact and understanding, so there is nothing to prevent these aerial creatures instructing each other in matters which seem mystery to terrestrial man.

Nor can I believe that avian migration, over distances which in the aggregate can be vast, is difficult except for hazards of weather. Like men, the bird has no magic power of orientation, and its physical and mental processes differ only in degree from any other creature. But the fact that so small and fragile a creature travels thousands of miles between spring and spring has pathos appealing to the imagination, so poetry and beauty spring from the human heart. Actuality is in the bird's, for it sees no marvel in the complex ecology and interdependent natural laws governing its universe.

The swallow knows no winter. As a tribe it inhabits all Europe throughout a summer which follows them across the world as they steer for the equator and reach towards Capricorn. It is with them as they flash blue wings in the November sky of the High Veldt and Great Karoo. Through the heat of December they soar above the houses of Capetown. With February they are flying north again, following the tide of rejuvenation that will bring them presently to springtime in England.

I have watched them on their way in early March, flying rapturously the radiant sky of Greece, and seen the sunlight paint their wings with richer blue then I had ever known before. So light and joyous was the beat with which they flew that none could have imagined they already had traversed two thousand miles across a savage continent to reach Aegean seas. They circled high above the golden columns of Athena's Temple, where the breeze throbbed deep music as though playing on the rigging of a ship. Then leisurely onwards, averaging twenty-five miles a day, journeying past Salamis whose tall hills lift bare above blue waters, skirting a dream-like shore where presently Mount Helicon looms serene and tall, and Delphi dreams; and soon enough the Straits of Missolonghi lead the swallows past the Ionian Isles of Zante and Cephalonia to the Adriatic Sea.

Three weeks later I had seen, from the battlemented Castello at Ascona, the vanguard of these birds come tilting and swerving over the mirrored reflection of the mountains in the smooth waters of Swiss Maggiore. A few days more and all the Alpine air was patterned and re-patterned with the swift erratic passage of their wings. But when I got to England the misty skies of April already knew them, and everywhere I heard the contented murmur of their nuptial song. Though by now I had seen spring in succession touch to flowering life the lands of Greece, and Italy, Switzerland and France, my heart in England stirred anew as if this was not only rebirth of my own land but my resurrection too.

17 Certayne Heronsewes

In the glowing sunlight of a warm and windless October afternoon I sailed the serene sky of Somerset, scanning the broad green
plains for sign of the world of long ago. So silken the air and so
slow the flight of my quietly humming aeroplane that time was
stilled, until it could no longer be counted in minutes but became
a smooth broad ocean, whose beginning reached beyond the
farthest horizon of my imagining. There was a spell about it which
transformed the ground below me, so that the unending rectangles
of dyke-framed meadowland showed, through their shape of
today, the pattern of many yesterdays.

Cupped between the long escarpment of the Mendips to the
north and the Poldens to the south were the shallow contours of
what was a lake strewn land when Joseph of Arimathaea's thorn
first bloomed on Glastonbury Tor—that islanded green hill rising
abruptly from the water-moors as an unmistakable landmark
which scores of times has guided my winged way. Today I sought

no distant places. Through the gleaming haze of the whirling propeller, the green spread of water meadows held my eye. I was looking back in time at the land as it was when Iron-age man lived among the waterways—and further back still to when no man was there, and beavers gnawed at stunted alders, and the pelican flew on ragged wings through these same skies to dive like a plummet for fish which swam where now brown cattle browse.

In imagination I could see the first encroachment of the silver seawater and the gradual flooding that had followed, then, in the course of centuries, the land rising a little, leaving great lagoons, meres and treacherous swamps. Indeed, had I not in flood-time of recent years watched these same vast lakes fill their old places, obliterating the boundary ditches to become once again Mere Pool, Hachewere, Bordenwere, Lichlake, and the like that are named in ancient books? Certainly, many meres were here untamed and scarcely explored in the sixteenth century, but steadily they were reclaimed, until the last of them was drained in the time of George III. Even so, much of the land remained accessible only by boats using the long straight draining rhynes, for it was little more than a hundred years ago that the first stone road was laid across the grass-grown bed of these lost lakes.

No small part of the magic of flying is this unveiling of the world, to see it fair and harmonious, linking today with long gone yesterdays. Earthbound, one may know the aspect of a road skirted by tall hedgerows; but from the air field after field springs unexpectedly to view, and beyond is yet another hinterland of tree and field and hedge whose existence had never before been one's concern nor even contemplated. Yet farther than the farmost field a minute's flying brings another and another vista, with the promise of new worlds and fresh adventure. No wonder the great gods lived in the heights, for it is only there that the very foundations of the world can be discerned, and one finds in hill and rock and silted meadow the earth's form moulded by the flood of time. No more the encompassment of hedges, nor the foreshortened view closed in by little hills; here in the freedom of the sky is power to see not merely distance scored in miles, but history etched by passing years.

That is what I dreamed as the little open cockpit aeroplane flew on, silencing my ears, immuring me with its muttering hum, while the air flowed soft and thinly warm against my face. . . . Yet there was no doubt that far below my scarlet wings I could see faint marks, among the many-acred squares of grass, that showed where long gone men had lived and fought and loved.

Tended and tilled though the Somerset water-moors have been for more than two hundred years, my sky view of the earth revealed ancient scars lightly hidden beneath the modern green—mute witness to the struggle of men, trying these many centuries to subdue the waterways and swamps. All the central area of meadowland lay smoothly flat, broken only by the intersecting lines of glittering ditches, but in the low rays of the autumn sun some of the outermost fields showed faintly lined and pitted, hint-ing at a different story from the one told by the overlay of recent trees and hedges. These were the rare indication, almost indistin-guishable from the ground, of ancient settlements, and near them were long gone rivulets and runnels graved in the modern turf as though it covered an estuary of mud from which the tide has ebbed.

I turned *Airymouse* a little, and, dropping lower, saw on the edge of the plain a sequestered triangle of field, scarred with shallow mounds. Ghosts of sixty circular houses these, which men, living a hundred years before Christ was born, built on an island they had made with logs and clay among the swamps. Simple though their life might be, they were skilled at least as greatly as any village community of today. They had craftsmen-smiths; woodworkers and turners; made implements of iron, or carts and boats; the potter at his eternal wheel moulded many a pleasing patterned jar and bowl, and women carded cloth with reindeer combs, played with their children, or cooked at ovens whose smoke writhed upward in the huts before finding escape through a hole in the roof.

From my vantage point in the high sky I could see it all again; the cluster of domed dwellings like an African *kraal*, blue-hazed with smoke; the palisade of wood ringing the huts around; boats moored by a jetty in the channel that is now a little brook—and the water sparkling calm and clear, where fishermen waited, poised with a spear, silent as herons tensed to strike.

The aeroplane curved further round, murmuring above the fields that hid all yesterday. The Mendip range spun slowly away to disappear behind my tail-plane and the Tor of Glastonbury again loomed ahead, dominating all the eastward view. Near its foot, tremmelled now within high banks, wound the river that long ago spread broad waters for a highway on which the Somerset abbots sailed their ships to lands beyond the lakes and swamps.

Airymouse went humming on, serene and sure in the sunlight, winged with magic, weaving spells that made romance of yester-day. I watched the slowly changing pattern of the dykes and fields with appraising eye, and, even as I looked, saw lightly scored in the near-by grass a great rectangle bisected by a modern rhyne. From each corner, scarcely showing, were diagonal lines that met the faint trace of another rectangle within the first. No fortress this, no camp enclosure or cattle compound, but the pipes and banks of a duk-decoy that had been gone a hundred years.

I slanted down to look closer. The wind whistled shriller round my head while the mist-blue horizon of Wessex dropped lower and lower until the landscape assumed an encompassing and intimate perspective. The narrow ditches dividing field from field showed their true size, becoming long canals of muddy water too wide for any horse to jump. Even the baize-like grass changed to rough herbage, tussocked and brittle. Each field grew broad enough to absorb the moment's vision, where before there had been half a county and two thousand years of history as easily comprehensible.

With soft sighing from the slipstream the aeroplane skimmed engineless the last few feet above the grass. As it drifted over the phantom decoy, long wings lifted from the ground in every direction: grey wings, pointed, patting the air with firm light beat—wings of large birds. Five pairs, twelve, sixteen materialized with startling suddenness as I swung the aeroplane abruptly round and opened the engine. The sky seemed full of them.

Tightly the aeroplane made its circle, climbing a little, engine roaring, shattering the illusion of quietness. Fields and ditches spun steadily round—then once more the time-smoothed mark of the decoy lay just ahead, and above it a cluster of small grey shadows flecked the air, becoming in the blink of an eyelid great birds streaming to left and right beneath my wings. There was a fleeting impression of heads drawn close to shoulders, and short tails stiffly spread yet seeming inadequate to counterpoise the play of forces on such wide wings. Light grey, with slate-blue pinions, the birds were revealed clear against the grass, flashing snow-white undersides as they steeply banked away. For one incredulous second I had believed them geese, but in the next realized with no less astonishment that they were herons. Not that it was surprising to find them here, but never previously had they been encountered more than one by one at the set intervals of their fishing beats along the length of rhyne and stream. Yet here they grouped in close gragarious company, for within the confines of the dried and crumbling decoy there must have been at least a score disturbed by my intruding aeroplane.

I circled, and watched them heading north and south, east and west, away and away in urgent flight that quickle settled to more leisured beating and flexing of their long wings. They were soon gone—and when I had turned about, however much I looked, there were only empty fields.

It should have been easy to find the distinctive grey of the flying herons above the meadow greens. Perhaps I did not search enough, for many times my aeroplane has followed single herons with ease, flying wing to wing, until I had come to know their breed almost intimately. Had we not circled high in summer skies, lifting easily in great bubbles of heated air? On other days we had skimmed the floods, putting to sudden flight the host of wintering wildfowl. From my aeroplane I had watched herons stiff-legged in the shallows ready to strike with deadly beak at eel or vole, and once I had seen the speared captive taken to the middle of a field lest it escape execution by sliding back into the stream.

I did not search either hard or long, for my thoughts were

preoccupied with other things. The past held me in thrall, and instead of the birds of today I could only imagine their forefathers far away back in the primitive mist of time.

I climbed a little, and looked down. . . . There was the decoy, its faint outline clear for me to see but meaningless now to those few who walk its nigh-unsuspected banks. Yet what a story might be told.

There was the decoy, a thousand feet below my wings—and where it lay was once the edge of Mere Pool, that great waterway, reed fringed, above which much stranger birds had flown in centuries long ago, and where men of the lake-villages had angled fish with hooks of bone. The years had fallen like autumn leaves, bearing all that life away, leaving only the traces of buried huts, a handful of bone and scattered shards. Yet the lake had remained. It was still there nine hundred years after the last Iron-age Celt had gone, for Abbot Dunstan owned it then, and for six hundred years more it stayed the property of the Glastonbury monks.

That was it! Herons and monks! As I climbed higher still above the many acres of rich pasture-land which now filled the emptied Pool of Mere, there came to mind, a little uncertainly at first, the words of a Sixteenth Century inventory, made when at last Glastonbury Abbey suffered dissolution and its ancient fabric was left to ruin:

> *Also there ys apperteyning unto the sayde manor one fysshing called the Mere which ys in circuite five myles and one myle and an halfe brode, wherein are great abundance of pykes, tenches, roches, and yeles, and of dyvers other kyndes of fyshes. . . . Also there ys a game of swannes apperteyning unto the same water. . . . Also there were viewed at this present survey certayne heronsewes, which have always used to brede there, to the number of iiii.*

Had I not just seen their descendents, the herons of four hundred years later, gathered at the site of their ancestral waters—and was it not probable that the nigh vanished decoy was one of these very same 'heronsewes to the number of iiii'?

Slowly I flew homeward, held in a dream, while the quiet fields of Somerset one by one drifted and vanished under my wings, like the notes of a song without words. I thought of all the happiness *Airymouse* had given me. She had done more than I dared hope three years ago, on my sunset hill. The sky world had been restored to me, and from it I could possess the earth. I was content.

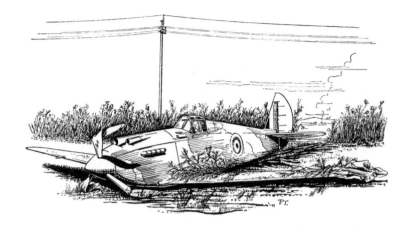

18 The Unknown God

A shimmering stillness hung over Merryfield, yet the quiet air seemed to rustle and murmur and sing the life of the wilderness—that spirit no longer man's; that sound of the seasons moving on tiptoe: the ceaseless, restless whisper of eager little wings and questing feet; the tinkle of stream and sleepy unwinding of rivers; the creak of trees stretching their limbs; the ruffling corn and sighing grass; the quiet flow of the summer breeze. I sat there listening, while I rested from the familiar struggle of opening the tall rusted door that hid *Airymouse*.

My tenancy had expired, and the Air Ministry were adamant that it could not be renewed. This was the last flight, and would take us to new quarters at Spreadeagle Hill, thirty miles eastward on the edge of the downlands overlooking the folds and forests of Cranbourne Chase. In many ways I was sorry to go. Even though the echoing hangars of Merryfield had long been deserted, and the great concrete runways were green with weed and grass at every joint and crack, it had always been a happy place.

THE UNKNOWN GOD

War had carved it from a quietude of peaceful meadows farmed by long generations of Somerset men who cared not tuppence for fame, but solely for their way of life, free of disturbance. Only once in the previous hundred years prior to World War II had outside events intruded, when an attempt was made at cutting through the Wessex peninsular with a great canal between Bridgwater and Lyme Regis to link the Bristol and English Channels—but before it could be completed came the revolutionary disturbance of railroad making. The now deserted track still ran alongside the aerodrome, intersecting one of the incomplete segments of the canal. Even so, the hurrying footsteps of townsfolk and their commerce had made no impact; an air of sovereign harmony and stillness surrounded Merryfield. Neither war nor naked destiny ever had alarmed it. Even in moments of great peril it seemed a haven— a place of safety and peace for which one gambled with fate, in hope that was almost certainty, in order to reach it.

In the years of the Second World War many a man had felt the sweeping relaxation of relief as the wheels of his aeroplane rasped onto the edge of Merryfield's long western runway and told with certainty that he and his comrades were safe. I remembered the white Wellington of Coastal Command which had come creeping cautiously in on the last of its fuel after a long patrol over a gale torn sea. It was a revealing moment to see the crew climb stiffly down and stand on the tarmac drinking in the peace and beautiful reality of Merryfield as they unclipped their parachute buckles before stumbling away to report. During another fragment of war I had watched Americans fly in with their wounded, and heard a lad with blood-stained arm mutter: 'Geeze! It's great to be back in the quiet.' And there were more personal memories. Twice I had just managed to reach it—each time with the complex engine of my prototype fighter useless, and the eight great paddle blades of its double propeller angled into an accidental airbrake of such tremendous resistance that it necessitated a glide steeper than a high pitched roof to avert the fatal peril of lost speed.

History has marched across these hidden acres on tiptoe, leaving only the concrete runways and black sheds as stark reminder of the destructive uselessness of war. Presently they will go, and future generations may see only quiet fields beneath skies which once knew the press of many wings. Looking around, I thought how inconceivable it was that our inescapable fate is to become involved in the struggle of powers beyond ourselves and our control. We die unknown and unmourned to vindicate a theory. We see our only heritage and the very reason for our life, this world of ours, laid waste at the behest of subscribers to ideologies of which we are utterly indifferent. Armies perish because self interest of the individual is mistaken for welfare of the whole. Yet the real battles are within man's soul where the search for spiritual deliverance is never stilled. Deep in us, we need to live by the conception of ultimate truth—and maybe die for it if necessary. Tragedy is when men die for the false conception of other men. As I pondered these things I began to perceive that even the lyrical peacefulness of Merryfield was fringed with unseen fire and unborn thunder. Slowly it became the soft hollow rumble and thud of the hangar doors as the breeze gently shook them—and gradually I opened my eyes to the warm brightness of the sun.

Ten minutes later *Airymouse* was winging down the runway for the last time. In a gentle climbing turn she rounded the familiar wood at the end. As we headed towards the new, through a beckoning world of light in which the dimension of aerial depth had been added without strangeness or questioning, it was impossible to realize that this was farewell to yet another chapter. In my sky world of winged motion the act of living takes new aspect, as though one walks the stage for a scene that is part of the endless passage of experience. I looked down at the fair earth with sense of compassionate protection, watching it broaden far beyond the daily enclosure of my dependence, until it became an arena set for the march Titans: yet the gods are ghosts, and it is ant-like invisible man who possesses the land and scrawls across it the mark of his relentless habitation.

Time and time again these skies have lured me to watch the unfolding scenes of England. Why does it so enthrall? Is it the revelation of vast encompassment by my mortal eye? In the broad expanse of sky my passing wings are anonymous. I am unseen, and therefore unconsidered, as I watch the minute to minute life of man and beast living their insignificant yet individually all consuming part in the frantic race to live ere they become the past. No sense of prying invades my consciousness. There, far below, is man releasing and manipulating huge natural forces in order to bolster his ever encroaching power—yet everywhere he builds refuges of mind and material to shield him from the intrusion of other human contacts. Perhaps some here and there wake up to dream, and turn their dreams to beneficient reality; some plumb the depths and never scale the heights; a few live with eager expectancy, finding happiness everywhere awaiting, and they are the lucky hostages to fortune.

Every land throughout the world mirrors to the sky a highly individual reflection of its mood of struggle or repose arising from its geological shaping and the spirit of its people. Except for huge areas that are untamable, the earth is engraved throughout its length and breadth by the effort of man to extract subsistence from field or factory; so the historical effect of his thought and action, as well as their current practical expression, seems visible to those who fly.

Today the simple pattern of small grazing fields beneath the scything wings of *Airymouse* gave place, after a few minutes flight, to a familiar plain of larger, well cultivated areas, stretching across a low tableland distantly bounded on south and east by ranging hills. In the glitter of sun beyond my starboard wing I saw the familiar landmarks of Windwhistle, Castle Hill, Seaborough, High Stoy, Crook Hill, and Penwood, set as intervals along the heights like trusty sentinels of long acquaintance. And dead ahead, the great oolitic hill of Ham rose straight-topped and sheer, above the Somerset fields. Up there was the ancient territory of the outlying Durotriges, who once lived on the hilltop in the biggest of all Iron-age forts in Britain, guarded on three sides by unscalable ditches. But their battles are long over: except for a thin infusion in our veins their race has vanished. Where their huts and palisades once stood, the Romans presently quarried the gold hued stone from the orange earth of the western side; and their successors, digging deeper, began to make the great rock beds yield the beautiful high towered churches, mullioned manor houses, and the thatched cottages found everywhere in Somerset and the Dorset border.

It was at the edge of the tableland below this western wall of Ham Hill, in a cornfield above which *Airymouse* was flying at this moment, that I had ended another almost disastrous flight. The second year of World War II was gathering momentum, and one of our tasks was to armour the low-wing single-seater Curtiss fighters which Britain was buying from the U.S.A. Their engines had been inhibited to prevent corrosion during transhipment across the Atlantic, but the compound proved difficult to remove and, coupled with inexperience in adjusting the boost of these engines, gave repeated difficulty, three times causing forced-landings. The last was the worst. I had taken off towards the distinctively coned hill of Montacute, two miles westward under the narrow eastern escarpment of Ham. As I left the airfield, power began to fade. Too low to turn, and with the ground ahead impossible for landing, I tried to gain what height I could in forlorn hope of clearing railway and main road and reaching somewhat more open fields. At a hundred feet, still with rows of trees fencing each small meadow, the engine began alternately dropping to insufficient power for flight and then briefly picking up. With each burst I would win a few feet, only to lose all I had gained, affording speed barely sufficient to prevent stalling and consequent catastrophic dive to ground. Soon I dropped slightly below the tree-tops, threading my way in the narrow open space above the curving railroad, on tenterhooks to thrust the nose into each passing field should the engine completely fail. On the outskirts of the clustered houses of Montacute village I was looking, up instead of down the slopes of its tower crowned hill, praying the engine would last until I drew past the great cliff of Ham itself, for beyond it some of the fields were bigger. The kicks of the engine grew feebler; speed was critical; height so slight that I passed between two trees. Any moment a pile-up was inevitable—yet each little field as it flicked into view was not only unsuitable, but seen too late to get the machine into the right position for a belly-landing. One needs a few seconds to gauge the glide so that the machine comes in at the marginally correct speed only a few inches above the leeward hedge.

Stoke-sub-Hamdon, nestling under the great fortress hill, dragged by with the machine still just airborne. Gingerly I edged the Curtiss across the main road beyond the last straggling houses only to find the immediate fields unsuitable, for one of the largest had been planted with a new orchard, and the other big one was on rising ground where I could not clear the boundary obstructions. But I could see a line of alders marking the brook-like course of the immature River Parret, where sometimes we used to swim. I knew that just beyond it were open level fields which could be my salvation if only I could reach them.

Instead, disaster blocked the way. The fighter was just 20 feet high—and there, right across my path, marched a low line of secondary power cables set on wooden poles. To pull up the nose to surmount them would be fatal, for the machine was flying only 10 m.p.h. above the stall—too slow even to make a proper glide. I snatched back the throttle, crammed down the nose, and dived at the ground to get under them, very conscious that it was a 50:50 chance the tall fin astern would touch the lowest wires. At that critical instant the engine stopped. With neither speed nor power to clear a tall blackthorn hedge preceding the poles, the machine plunged through the thicket as I levelled off, and an instant later the almost stationary propeller blades folded like sunflower petals as they scraped the ground beneath the low power lines. With a jolting jar the belly of the machine hit the earth, flinging me into the windscreen despite the tightly pulled straps of my safety harness. In a slight daze I sat there, blood oozing from my helmet where my forehead had been scalped—but at least we had avoided electrocution.

A long time ago, all that. Today *Airymouse* waved her wings at the scene of that lucky forced-landing as she gently circuited, then crossed the little river where willows frame the pool in which

we used to dive. Serenely she hummed onward, heading south of
the hollow hiding Yeovil's spreading houses. Soon the Dorset
Heights ranged across the farthest skyline. Behind them lay lands
created in the dawn of living things, but the bold contours of
Pilsden Pen and Lewsdon Hill hid the antiquities of Marshwood
Vale and the fossil stratified sea-cliffs from Charmouth to Lyme.
Between me and the hills the quiet meadows of Blackmore Vale
began to reach eastward, with Batcombe Down rising boldly
above them, Bulbarrow in the distance, and beyond that fortress
hill the steep bluffs of Wooland and Bell Hill swept diagonally
northward. All this high land of the ancients had lain almost
unchanged for generation after generation of men with quieter
minds than those suffering the megalomania and tyranny of cities
today. On these chalk downs, higher and nobler even that those
of Sussex, the mark of prehistoric occupation was everywhere:
ditches, outlines of fields, settlements and trackways. Yet steadily
the plough has been encroaching in recent years. All the secret
places will soon be gone, and the rumble of tractors echo where
only the wind whispered among grass and gorse undisturbed by
plough for two thousand years.

Even as *Airymouse* gently began to bank towards the downs my
eye was drawn from the distances to a quiet, sunlit meadow
beneath her turning wing that hid another story etched tragically
across my middle years. All of visible significance was this small
square field and its evident proximity to another narrow strip of
elm fringed meadow hard by a pretty country lane descending
from a shallow hill. Instantly the very air around me seemed
sadness as I remembered that far day of sunny autumn. Suddenly
the crash alarm had begun stridently clanging on the airfield
Control Tower. Fire tender and ambulance hurried from their
open sheds. I knew two of our fighters were up on test. One was a
difficult prototype. I was filled with foreboding. What had happened? Which was in trouble? Urgently I rang, but controllers
and ground crews were too busy to answer the telephone. I raced
downstairs, only to meet Alan running up to me. 'They've had a
radio message,' he said. 'Pete is down south by east of here.'

'Is he all right?'

'A naval two-seater signalled that one of ours could be seen going down—they know nothing more.'

Pete had been on a photographic mission and was unlikely to have run out of fuel, so either the propeller or engine must have again given trouble. Knowing how great were the odds against a safe forced-landing in that area, Alan and I dashed to the helicopter he had just finished flying. Within three minutes we were away, accompanied by a nurse and first aid man with their equipment, heading south by east across impossibly small fields—searching, searching as we climbed. The first run as far as Bulbarrow drew a blank. The second was more south. The hundreds of square miles visible in every direction seemed empty, but as we turned back I saw a lazily drifting column of smoke five miles away. Alan and I looked at each other in consternation. The blackness of that pencil line was ominous. Three desperate minutes, and we were above burning wreckage scattered across the corner of a short and narrow field. A moment later the helicopter touched down close to the pall of evil smoke coiling from the smashed fuselage—and we knew Peter had gone for ever.

Five years later his young wife learned to fly. Late one summer evening she was piloting a Tiger Moth from Wiltshire to her flying club near Exeter after assurance of suitable weather. Having completed more than half the journey through sunlit skies a local thunderstorm loomed across her course, so she turned south, intending to follow the coast to the Exe estuary but found it impossible. Hemmed by low cloud, she decided to find my home aerodrome and wait there rather than risk flying over the high ground westward, but presently spotting a field bigger than the rest, thought an immediate landing wiser. It was the first she attempted away from the wide expanse of an aerodrome, but after a cautious circuit the Tiger Moth rumbled gently over the eastern hedge, heading into the evening breeze, and touching down with the aplomb of a professional, came to a stop a good 100 yards before reaching the further hedge, Pilot and passenger walked to the nearby village, reported to the police, then 'phoned me for advice and help.

Today, as I looked down from my little red aeroplane, there below was that same square, tufty field she had used—so small that only in direst emergency would I attempt it. And there, at the point where she started her approach, was that other fateful strip of tree surrounded meadow I had never dared show her— where our youthful, gallant Pete had met his end. 'They shall not grow old, as we that are left grow old,' I silently prayed. 'Age shall not weary them, nor the years condemn. At the going down of the sun, and in the morning, we will remember them.'

I gathered *Airymouse* and edged her away. We headed once more towards those looming Dorset Heights, where great herds of sheep, with their nomadic shepherds, roamed fifty years ago, grazing the sweet turf; but today it was as though Arcadia, unaware of tragedies, was sleeping under the noon-tide sun. On these great hills, created long before man evolved, nothing stirred.

Winging a broad curve, I rediscovered many places where time still held its hand. Presently I throttled back and went gliding down in murmuring silence to alight on that same turfy hill-spur where I made my own first open-country landing half a lifetime back. *Airymouse* settled lightly as a bird. I switched off the engine, climbed out, and half expectantly gazed around. It was a world of smooth green turf and wide expanse of sky, with the unforgettable downland air carrying the mingled perfumes of many flowers. Nothing seemed changed, but in the quietness I heard faint stirring: a sigh, yawn, rasp of hoof. A satyr-head lifted, and the sun lit on swept-back horns and face with high arched nose and pointed ears, revealing a torso painted like copper, but with thighs hidden by the hill-slope. . . . For a long time the figure remained immobile, staring down the tumbled hillside, gazing far across the shimmer of the plain, as though brooding in sadness, dreaming of the world when it was young. There had been songs, dances, night-long revels; stars and fire; hair flying in the moonlight; the chase, laughter, sobs; a shadowed upturned face. With quizzical expectancy he gazed around, as though at any instant old comrades would appear. Satyr's and fauns might come prancing across the hill slopes, their laughter quick to catch the echo of his; and the nymphs would come like moths, fluttering, fluttering to the candlelight . . . Where had they gone? Why was he deserted? Had they grown old with the world, wearied, and left him? Did they sleep, deep in the last sleep, leaving him alone and immortal? Did they sleep—or was he forgotten?

With a short coughing laugh that echoed across the fields, this reincarnation of Pan shattered the silence. As he lifted his head I saw him more clearly. In a moment he was joined by others: horned sheep in scores, sheep in hundreds; slowly moving as they grazed . . . Was this a last jest of the gods in a place they once loved?

I turned to *Airymouse,* spun her propeller, and climbed aboard. As we rushed across the shorn grass the sheep slowly scattered, and rooks rose on ponderous wings. I looked down at the little field. It was unlikely I would ever go there again—yet it was another farewell I would refuse to make absolute, for there would remain awareness that this Arcadian hill, like Avalon and Merryfield and all other places of earlier significance, would be waiting a mere retraceable step behind my new horizons of the Dorset chalk-hills. Within the history of their long centuries they had already added the brief passage of my earlier days and made it invisible to all except me.

Climbing steadily, I set *Airymouse* across the wooded heights of Melbury Bubb and headed towards the ditched fortress of lofty Bulbarrow where its foothill jutted a tree-clad promontory from the northern face of the sweeping upland ridge. Presently we were at 1,500 feet, humming through clear blue sky that revealed vast distances. Through the whirl of the black propeller, I could see that the great chalk heights stretched to where I knew Winchester must be, and if I turned *Airymouse* a little, I could see the Devon hills dwarfed far back in the opposite direction. Northward lay the long blue line of the Mendips; south and nearer rose the bold Purbecks, with a silvered sea behind St Aldhelm's Head, and the Isle of Wight looming magically beyond the mirror-smooth waters of Poole harbour. Down there, by the rivers and marshes, was the newest of Dorset's land, co-eval with her first men; all else was infinitely long established before the first human voice was heard. In keeping with my thoughts I had subconsciously ruddered, watching the southward view, and my returning gaze fell on an area of pine-studded heaths and patchwork fields where Whirl-wind fighters had been based while conducting low-level cross-Channel sorties in the early years of the Second World War. Their young pilots staunchly believed in the virtue of these machines, for if one of the twin-engines was hit by *flak* they could still return in safety using the other. Many times I watched the squadron take off, and waited in hope that all would return—but with devastating frequency yet another high spirited young man would be missing, and we hid our desolation at the relentless sacrifice of war when man's true entitlement was peace and the fulfilment of his days.

Too small and unsuitably placed for later operations, this air-field was presently closed and I saw it no more until I made an emergency landing there after the war. Flying the first of a new type of massive fighter powered with the last and biggest piston-engine made by Rolls before they turned to turbines, I was at 16,000 feet—the countryside lost beneath a great strata of cloud which covered all Wessex except the Dorset coastline—when, with no warning, the engine cut cold. Even had we equipment for radio fixes, it would have been useless because there was no established aerodrome near enough to which I might be directed. Either I had to eject myself for a parachute drop or take the marginal chance of finding a field for a belly-landing when I broke through cloud only 3,000 feet above the earth with less than a minute to go before touching. Then I remembered Warmwell of the war-time Whirlwinds. It offered a slight chance of saving this costly prototype on which its manufacturer's future so much depended. Because the southern end of the great cloud stratus was fringed by familiar coastline I could gauge from the angles sub-tended by St Albans Head, Lulworth and Portland that I was not far from Dorchester; so Warmwell must be only a few miles farther on. Every second counted, for my ominously silent fighter was dropping like a brick as we headed towards a hazy blue indentation which I hoped must signify a small gap in the vast white floor of cloud.

Two minutes later the machine reached it, and by a miracle I caught a glimpse, through the ragged rift, of tall radio towers which I knew were south of Dorchester. Cloud vapour swirled round the wings, darkened momentarily as the machine plunged through to find a drabbly shadowed, dispirited world beneath—and lo! a second miracle had happened: a few miles ahead was the open space of Warmwell. By fantastic chance the fighter's thunderbolt gliding angle seemed just sufficient to let me reach it, though it was touch and go whether, through lack of a few feet of height, I was going to crash into the copse on the nearest boundary. The landscape rushed up engulfingly—but when the bulky fighter was no more than a hundred feet above the trees, I suddenly knew that we had made it by inches. I tugged at the emergency levers and shot down undercarriage and flaps. Even as the legs locked home the wheels rasped through waist-high grass. With the machine jolting ever slower along the length of the airfield I sat back with the glorious feeling that we were safe.

When the rescue team found me a couple of hours later, one of the cars collided with a stump of concrete hidden by the tall grass. A moment later they found another, and another. Quickly it became apparent that the entire area was thickly patterned with hundreds of great concrete blocks which had been set up during the closure of the airfield to prevent German gliders landing if invasion was attempted.

'Just your blind luck!' grinned the foreman. 'Your wheel tracks go right through the lot—within inches of some—and it is all of a 1,200 yard run!'

As I reheaded *Airymouse,* these many years later, towards her new Dorset home, I thought how greatly luck had been with me throughout my flying career: the fortunate cat with ninety-nine lives—yet you and you who were so close were taken long before your time.

By now the Stone-age fort of Bulbarrow, heavily encircled with defensive ditches where many an earlier youth had died in pre-historic times, was passing 1,000 feet beneath my wheels. Steadily we climbed. The last of Blackmoor Vale spread wide beneath the great eyebrow of downland curving towards massive Hambledon Hill and the long meridianal ridge of high land that makes the western boundary of Cranbourne Chase. Only a little further to go. Beyond those heights were renewed horizons which I would some day re-explore from my aeroplane's new home.

Long before the advent of jets so swift that they traverse all Wessex in five minutes, I often lingered, with one or other of the slow flying machines of those earlier days, above the sweeping downlands of Dorset and Hampshire while I studied the story of their ancient ways. Today, tomorrow, or next year, from the windswept cockpit of *Airymouse* I might still be able to look back on the morning of the world. Dappled shadows of summer cumulus would sweep across those almost vanished signs of man's early handiwork, made when first he patiently began to till the earth. Forgotten paths, straight lined enclosures, hut circles, pits, long lost villages, would be discerned everywhere etched faintly in turf and plough, yet indelible through the ages. As I hover above the rolling acres, they will again disclose, stanza by stanza, the shadowed moods of mankind's endeavour and despair. Like the sound of a vesper bell the theme will drift upward, and I shall rediscover the unchanging lesson that it is not the political leader and his theories, nor the tycoon amassing gold, or the soldier at arms, but the heart of man beating to the heart of woman that spins the world.

I began to turn *Airymouse* in a last great curve until the sun was at her tail. Three miles ahead, the high hills of my destination beckoned, guarding a land which saw little of the Roman, and was long in peaceable possession of the Iron-age farmers. Here would be new adventure above the unchanging beauty of ancient ways. Once more the Phoenix flame was leaping from the ashes.